PATH TO A QUALITY TRADER

经贸强国之道

庆祝改革开放 40 周年

中华人民共和国商务部 编

中国商务出版社
CHINA COMMERCE AND TRADE PRESS

图书在版编目（CIP）数据

经贸强国之道：庆祝改革开放 40 周年 / 中华人民共和国商务部编 . —— 北京：中国商务出版社，2018.12
ISBN 978-7-5103-2663-9

Ⅰ .①经… Ⅱ .①中… Ⅲ .①对外贸易 – 成就 – 中国 Ⅳ .① F752

中国版本图书馆 CIP 数据核字 (2018) 第 251485 号

经贸强国之道
——庆祝改革开放 40 周年

Path to a Quality Trader：Celebrating Four Decades of Reform and Opening up

中华人民共和国商务部 编

出　　版：中国商务出版社
地　　址：北京市东城区安定门外大街东后巷 28 号　　邮编：100710
责任部门：国际经济与贸易事业部（010-64269744　bjys@cctpress.com）
项目统筹：张高平
责任编辑：张永生　何　昕　李彩娟
封面题字：廖以厚
责任校对：龚利霞　卓文娟
装帧设计：刘之君
图片来源：商务部、新华社、视觉中国、东方 IC、北京商务委、服务外包杂志社、承包商会、刘冬平、李松、厉宝骏、任锡海等

总 发 行：中国商务出版社发行部（010-64266119）
网购零售：010-64269744
网　　址：http://www.cctpress.com
邮　　箱：cctp@cctpress.com

印　　刷：廊坊市蓝海德彩印有限公司
开　　本：889 毫米 × 1194 毫米　1/12
印　　张：19　　　　　　　字　　数：210 千字
版　　次：2018 年 12 月第 1 版　　印　　次：2018 年 12 月第 1 次印刷
书　　号：ISBN 978-7-5103-2663-9
定　　价：280.00 元

商务部庆祝改革开放 40 周年画册
编辑委员会

主　　　　任　钟　山

副　主　任　钱克明

委 员 单 位　办公厅　政研室　综合司　条法司　财务司　外贸司

　　　　　　服贸司　外资司　合作司　贸易救济调查局　国际司

　　　　　　世贸司　亚洲司　西亚非洲司　欧亚司　欧洲司

　　　　　　美大司　台港澳司　电子商务司　外事司　机关党委

　　　　　　研究院

编辑部主任　顾学明

编辑部副主任　于广生　郭周明

高 级 顾 问　尹艳林　隆国强　裴长洪　李　钢　张燕生　赵忠秀

采 编 人 员　张高平　张永生　何　昕　李彩娟　郝宝生　刘冬平

文 稿 撰 写　何　昕　张高平

英 文 翻 译　商务部外事司翻译处

序

　　1978 年党的十一届三中全会召开，拉开了改革开放的序幕。习近平总书记指出，改革开放是党和人民大踏步赶上时代的重要法宝，是坚持和发展中国特色社会主义的必由之路。四十年来，中国抓住经济全球化的机遇，坚持对外开放不停滞、不动摇，自力更生、鼎新图强、砥砺前行，创造了经济增长的奇迹。

　　今天，中国已是世界第二大经济体、货物贸易第一大国，吸引外资多年保持全球第二位，服务贸易、对外投资跃居全球第二位。2008 年国际金融危机爆发以来，中国对世界经济增长贡献率年均超过 30%，成为世界经济增长的主要稳定器和动力源，为促进世界和平与发展作出了不可替代的贡献。

　　"一带一路"倡议为世界播撒下一粒粒希望的种子。2013 年以来，中国同沿线国家贸易投资合作稳步推进，一批重大基础设施和产能合作项目陆续落地。"一带一路"联通陆与海，交织古与今，新的历史画卷已然开启。

　　中国智慧与世界激荡，中国声音与世界交响。"一带一路"倡议、中国国际进口博览会、亚洲基础设施投资银行等一系列"中国方案"成为构建人类命运共同体的生动实践。

　　回望对外经贸历史，四十年锐意进取，四十年奋勇创新，四十年岁月峥嵘。习近平总书记指出，将改革开放进行到底，不断实现人民对美好生活的向往，在新时代创造中华民族新的更大奇迹。未来我们将继续坚定不移地走在改革开放的大路上，逢山开路，遇水搭桥，为实现"两个一百年"奋斗目标和中华民族伟大复兴的中国梦而作出更多贡献。愿祖国更加繁荣昌盛，山河长青！

商务部部长　钟山

二〇一八年十二月

Preface

The 3rd Plenary Session of the 11th CPC Central Committee in 1978 lifted the curtain on China's reform and opening up. President Xi Jinping notes that reform and opening up is an important instrument for the CPC and Chinese people to catch up with the times in great strides and the only way of adhering to and developing socialism with Chinese characteristics. In the ensuing four decades, China seized the opportunity of globalization and pursued opening up with perseverance, self-reliance and great vigor against all odds, creating a miracle of economic growth.

Today, as the world's 2nd largest economy and biggest trader in goods, China has been the world's No.2 FDI destination for many years and jumped to the 2nd place in terms of trade in services and ODI. Since the international financial crisis of 2008, China's contribution to world economic growth has averaged above 30% annually, making it a key anchor and engine of world economic growth with irreplaceable contributions to world peace and development.

The Belt and Road initiative has sowed a seed of hope for the world. Since 2013, China's trade and investment cooperation with countries along the routes has advanced steadily, as a host of key infrastructure and capacity cooperation projects get implemented successively, opening up a new historic chapter that connects the land with the sea, and the past with the present.

As Chinese wisdom spreads and voice echoed around the world, the Belt and Road initiative, the China International Import Expo and the Asian Infrastructure Investment Bank, among other Chinese propositions, have become vivid exercises to build a community of shared future for all mankind.

Four decades of pioneering enterprise, courageous innovation and hard struggle have carried us to this juncture to look back on the winding path of the great cause. President Xi Jinping calls for carrying through reform and opening up to continuously meet people's aspirations for a good life and create greater miracles of the Chinese nation in the new era. In the future, we will stay the course of reform and opening up, come what may, to contribute to the realization of the two centenary goals and the great renaissance of the Chinese nation. Prosperity and long life to our motherland!

Zhong Shan

Minister of Commerce

December, 2018

目　录

Contents

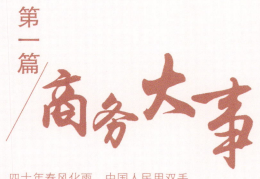

第一篇／**商务大事**

四十年众志成城，四十年砥砺奋进，四十年春风化雨，中国人民用双手书写了国家和民族发展的壮丽史诗。国家从贫困到富裕，从封闭到开放，一个个历史瞬间成就了改革开放的重大成果。

Part I   Landmark Economic Events

With four decades of unity and hard work, the Chinese people wrote the glorious history of their country's and their nation's development with their own hands. As the country rose from poverty to prosperity and from seclusion to openness, the historical moments were turned into the main achievements of reform and opening up.

7月，党中央、国务院决定在深圳、珠海、汕头和厦门试办特区。

3月，关贸总协定总理事会成立中国工作组，对所有缔约方开放。

7月，中国政府向关税与贸易总协定总干事提交关于恢复中国在关贸总协定缔约国地位的申请。

12月，中共十一届三中全会作出实行改革开放的重大决策。

5月，党中央、国务院正式将"特区"定名为"经济特区"。

7月，党中央、国务院批转《广东、福建两省和经济特区工作会议纪要》。

12月，党中央、国务院肯定试办特区3年来的成绩。

2月，党中央、国务院指出：长三角、珠三角、闽南厦漳泉三角地区应逐步形成贸—工—农型的生产结构，建立以外向型为主的经济。

5月，党中央、国务院决定进一步开放大连、天津、秦皇岛、烟台、青岛、连云港、南通、上海、宁波、温州、福州、广州、湛江、北海等14个沿海港口城市。

9月，党中央、国务院发布《关于加强利用外资工作的指示》。

1978 1979 1980 1981 1982 1983 1984 1985 1986 1987

In Dec. 1978, the Third Plenary Session of the Eleventh Central Committee of the Communist Party of China made a major decision to implement reform and opening up.

In Jul. 1979, the Central Committee of the Communist Party of China and the State Council decided to pilot special zones in Shenzhen, Zhuhai, Shantou and Xiamen.

In May. 1980, the Central Committee of the Communist Party of China and the State Council officially renamed the "special zones" to "special economic zones".

In Jul. 1981, the Central Committee of the Communist Party of China and the State Council endorsed the *Minutes of the Working Meeting on Guangdong and Fujian Provinces and the Special Economic Zones*.

In Dec. 1982, the Central Committee of the Communist Party of China and the State Council recognized the achievements of the pilot special zones over the past three years.

In Sep. 1983, the Central Committee of the Communist Party of China and the State Council published the *Instructions on Strengthening the Utilization of Foreign Capital*.

In May. 1984, the Central Committee of the Communist Party of China and the State Council decided to further open up 14 coastal port cities, including Dalian, Tianjin, Qinhuangdao, Yantai, Qingdao, Lianyungang, Nantong, Shanghai, Ningbo, Wenzhou, Fuzhou, Guangzhou, Zhanjiang and Beihai.

In Feb. 1985, the Central Committee of the Communist Party of China and the State Council pointed out that the Yangtze River Delta, the Pearl River Delta, and the Xiamen–Quanzhou–Zhangzhou Delta in South Fujian should gradually develop a trade–industry–agriculture production structure and establish an export–oriented economy.

In Jul. 1986, the Chinese government submitted an application to the Director–General of the General Agreement on Tariffs and Trade to restore China's status as a contracting party to the GATT.

In Mar. 1987, the GATT General Council established the China Working Group open to all parties.

4 月，七届全国人大一次会议正式批准设立海南省，划定海南岛为经济特区。

7 月，首届北京国际博览会在中国国际展览中心举行。

9 月，党的十五大报告提出：深化对外经济贸易体制改革，完善代理制，扩大企业外贸经营权，形成平等竞争的政策环境。

12 月，中国开始接受国际货币基金组织协定第八条款，实行人民币经常项目下的可兑换。

4 月，党中央、国务院决定开发和开放上海浦东新区。

6 月，中国成为世界贸易组织观察员。

5 月，八届全国人大常务委员会七次会议通过《对外贸易法》。

4 月，七届全国人大四次会议审议通过《外商投资企业和外国企业所得税法》。

1 月，邓小平视察深圳发表南方谈话，中国从此进入扩大开放的新阶段。

3 月，八届全国人大一次会议决定，对外经济贸易部更名为对外贸易经济合作部。

1988 **1989** **1990** **1991** **1992** **1993** **1994** **1995** **1996** **1997**

In Apr. 1988, the First Session of the Seventh National People's Congress officially approved the establishment of Hainan Province and designated Hainan Island as a special economic zone.

In Jul. 1989, the first Beijing International Exposition was held at the China International Exhibition Center.

In Apr. 1990, the Central Committee of the Communist Party of China decided to develop and open up the Shanghai Pudong New Area.

In Apr. 1991, the Fourth Session of the Seventh National People's Congress reviewed and approved the *Income Tax Law of the People's Republic of China for Enterprises with Foreign Investment and Foreign Enterprises*.

In Jan. 1992, Deng Xiaoping paid a visit to Shenzhen, where he made the southern tour speech. China has since entered a new stage of expanded opening up.

In Mar. 1993, the First Session of the Eighth National People's Congress decided that the Ministry of Foreign Economic Relations and Trade be renamed the Ministry of Foreign Trade and Economic Cooperation.

In May. 1994, the Seventh Session of the Standing Committee of the Eighth National People's Congress passed the *Foreign Trade Law*.

In Jun. 1995, China became an observer of the World Trade Organization.

In Dec. 1996, China accepted Article 8 of the Articles of Agreement of the International Monetary Fund, beginning RMB convertibility under the current account.

In Sep. 1997, the report to the Fifteenth National Congress of the Communist Party of China proposed to deepen the reform of the foreign economic and trade system, improve the agency system, expand the right to conduct foreign trade, and form a policy environment for equal competition.

10 月，中共十五届三中全会明确提出"走出去"。

3 月，国务院发布《关于进一步推进西部大开发的若干意见》，实施西部大开发战略。

4 月，第 101 届中国出口商品交易会更名为中国进出口商品交易会。

4 月，国务院发布《关于促进中部地区崛起的若干意见》，实施中部崛起战略。

10 月，中非合作论坛第一届部长级会议在中国北京举行。

10 月，中共十六届五中全会作出将天津滨海新区开发开放纳入国家发展战略布局的重大决策。

12 月，中国正式成为世界贸易组织第 143 个成员。

11 月，《中国—东盟全面经济合作框架协议》签署，标志着中国自由贸易区建设进程正式起步。

4 月，十届全国人大常务委员会八次会议修订通过新的《对外贸易法》。

6 月，中央政府与香港特区政府签署《内地与香港关于建立更紧密经贸关系的安排》。

In Oct. 1998, the Third Plenary Session of the Fifteenth Central Committee of the Communist Party of China clearly put forward the "going global" proposal.

In Mar. 1999, the State Council issued the *Several Opinions on Further Promoting the Development of the Western Regions* to launch the strategy to develop China's western regions.

In Oct. 2000, the first ministerial meeting of the Forum on China–Africa Cooperation (FOCAC) was held in Beijing, China.

In Dec. 2001, China officially became the 143rd member of the World Trade Organization.

In Nov. 2002, *Framework Agreement on Comprehensive Economic Cooperation between China and ASEAN* was signed, marking the start of China's FTA practice.

In Jun. 2003, the Central Government and the Hong Kong SAR Government signed the *Mainland and Hong Kong Closer Economic Partnership Arrangement*.

In Apr. 2004, the Eighth Session of the Standing Committee of the Tenth National People's Congress revised and adopted the new *Foreign Trade Law*.

In Oct. 2005, the Fifth Plenary Session of the Sixteenth Central Committee of the Communist Party of China made a major decision to include the development and opening up of Tianjin Binhai New Area in the planning of national development strategies.

In Apr. 2006, the State Council issued the *Several Opinions on Promoting the Rise of the Central Regions* to launch strategy of the rise of Central China.

In Apr. 2007, the 101st China Export Commodities Fair was renamed China Import and Export Fair.

2 月，国务院发布《关于同意推进境外经济贸易合作区建设意见的批复》，全面推进境外经济贸易合作区建设。

11 月，首届中国国际进口博览会在上海举办。

5 月，"一带一路"国际合作高峰论坛在北京举行。

5 月，首届海峡论坛在厦门、福州、莆田、泉州四地举行。

8 月，党中央、国务院决定设立中国辽宁、浙江、河南、湖北、重庆、四川、陕西自由贸易试验区。

6 月，海峡两岸签署《海峡两岸经济合作框架协议》。

12 月，亚洲基础设施投资银行在北京正式成立。

4 月，中国首次发布《中国的对外援助》白皮书。

3 月，商务部等十部委联合发布《关于加快转变外贸发展方式的指导意见》。

8 月，党中央、国务院决定设立中国上海自由贸易试验区。

12 月，党中央、国务院决定设立中国广东、天津、福建自由贸易试验区。

2008 2009 2010 2011 2012 2013 2014 2015 2016 2017 2018

In Feb. 2008, the State Council issued the *Reply on Agreeing to the Opinions on Promoting the Development of Overseas Trade and Economic Cooperation Zones* to comprehensively advance the development of overseas trade and economic cooperation zones.

In May. 2009, the first Straits Forum was held in Xiamen, Fuzhou, Putian and Quanzhou.

In Jun. 2010, the Cross-Strait *Economic Cooperation Framework Agreement* (ECFA) was signed.

In Apr. 2011, China released the first White Paper on *China's Foreign Aid*.

In Mar. 2012, MOFCOM and other 9 ministries jointly released the *Guiding Opinions for Accelerating the Transformation of Foreign Trade Development*.

In Aug. 2013, the CPC Central Committee and the State Council decided to establish the China (Shanghai) Pilot Free Trade Zone.

In Dec. 2014, the State Council decided to establish pilot free trade zones in Guangdong, Tianjin and Fujian.

In Dec. 2015, the Asian Infrastructure Investment Bank was established in Beijing.

In Aug. 2016, the CPC Central Committee and the State Council decided to establish pilot free trade zones in Liaoning, Zhejiang, Henan, Hubei, Chongqing, Sichuan and Shaanxi.

In May. 2017, the Belt and Road Forum for International Cooperation was held in Beijing.

In Nov. 2018, the first China International Import Expo was held in Shanghai.

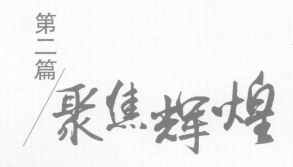

第二篇 / 聚焦辉煌

四十年间，中国经济以前所未有的速度实现跨越式发展，综合国力和国际影响力日益提升。当今中国已成为世界第二大经济体，进出口额居世界首位。

Part II　Focus on Brilliant Achievements

Over the past four decades, Chinese economy has developed by leaps and bounds at an unprecedented rate, building up its comprehensive national strength and international influence. China is the world's second largest economy and ranks first in import and export value.

第一章 数说中国对外经济贸易

Chapter 1 Foreign Trade and Economic Development in Numbers

改革开放 40 年来，中国人民艰苦奋斗、顽强拼搏，推动中国发生了翻天覆地的变化。中国已成为第一大货物贸易国、第二大服务贸易国；中国对外直接投资居全球第三，吸收外商直接投资全球排名第二。

Thanks to the persistent and hard work of the Chinese people in the past four decades since the inception of reform and opening up, China has undergone tremendous changes. It has become the largest trader in goods, the second largest trader in service, the third largest foreign direct investor and the second largest FDI recipient.

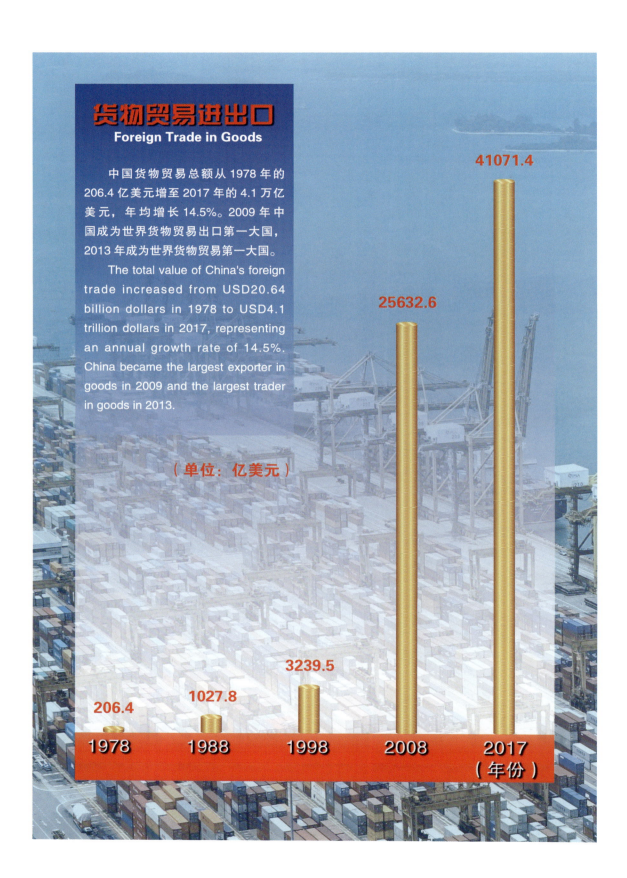

货物贸易进出口
Foreign Trade in Goods

中国货物贸易总额从 1978 年的 206.4 亿美元增至 2017 年的 4.1 万亿美元，年均增长 14.5%。2009 年中国成为世界货物贸易出口第一大国，2013 年成为世界货物贸易第一大国。

The total value of China's foreign trade increased from USD20.64 billion dollars in 1978 to USD4.1 trillion dollars in 2017, representing an annual growth rate of 14.5%. China became the largest exporter in goods in 2009 and the largest trader in goods in 2013.

（单位：亿美元）

41071.4

25632.6

3239.5

1027.8

206.4

1978　1988　1998　2008　2017
（年份）

贸易结构持续优化
Continuously Upgraded Trade Structure

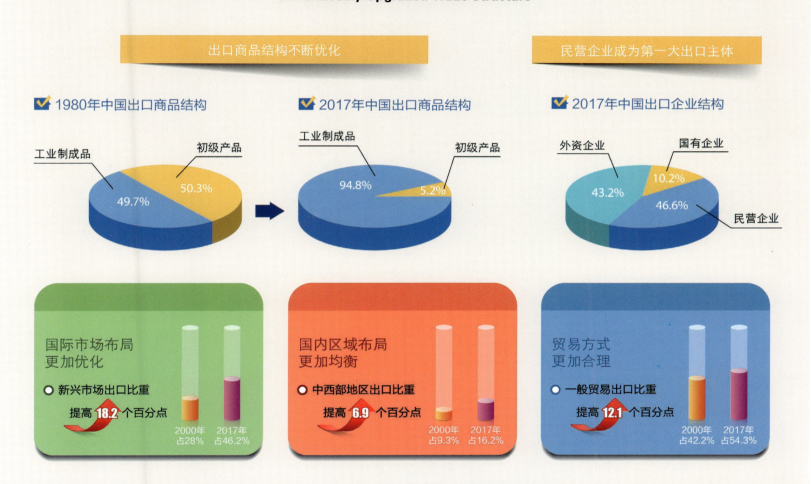

出口商品结构不断优化

民营企业成为第一大出口主体

☑ 1980年中国出口商品结构

☑ 2017年中国出口商品结构

☑ 2017年中国出口企业结构

工业制成品　初级产品
49.7%　50.3%

工业制成品　初级产品
94.8%　5.2%

外资企业　国有企业
43.2%　10.2%
46.6%　民营企业

国际市场布局
更加优化

● 新兴市场出口比重

提高 **18.2** 个百分点

2000年 占28%　2017年 占46.2%

国内区域布局
更加均衡

● 中西部地区出口比重

提高 **6.9** 个百分点

2000年 占9.3%　2017年 占16.2%

贸易方式
更加合理

● 一般贸易出口比重

提高 **12.1** 个百分点

2000年 占42.2%　2017年 占54.3%

改革开放以来，国际市场结构、国内区域布局、商品结构、经营主体、贸易方式更加优化。

Since the Reform and Opening-up, China's trade structure has been continuously upgraded in terms of international market layout, domestic regional distribution, commodity mix, foreign trade operators, and trade patterns.

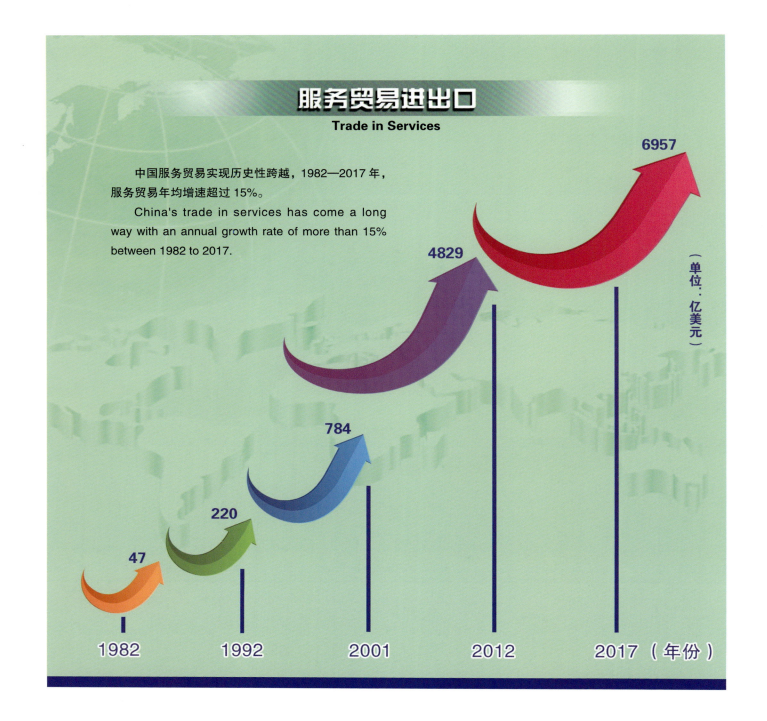

服务贸易进出口

Trade in Services

中国服务贸易实现历史性跨越，1982—2017 年，服务贸易年均增速超过 15%。

China's trade in services has come a long way with an annual growth rate of more than 15% between 1982 to 2017.

（单位：亿美元）

6957

4829

784

220

47

1982   1992   2001   2012   2017（年份）

服务贸易世界排名
China's Ranking in Trade in Services

1982 年，中国服务贸易进出口额占世界的 0.6%，位列全球第 34 位。2017 年，中国服务贸易进出口额占世界的 6.7%，位列全球第 2 位。

In 1982, the value of China's foreign trade in services accounted for 0.6% of the world, the 34th in the world; in 2017, it accounted for 6.7% of the world, the 2nd in the world.

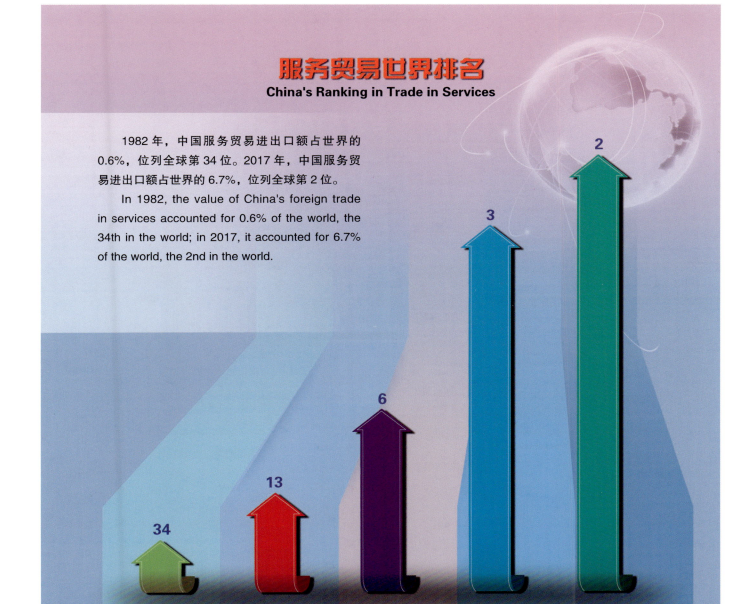

34　1982

13　1992

6　2001

3　2012

2　2017 （年份）

外商直接投资
Foreign Direct Investment (FDI)

中国利用外资从无到有，从有到优，规模位居全球第二，质量不断提升。

FDI coming to China rose from zero to the 2nd largest in the world, with ever–improving quality.

（单位：亿美元）

1363

1211

469

110

9

1983 1992 2001 2012 2017

（年份）

高技术产业利用外资
FDI Utilization in High-tech Industry

1998 年以来，外资不断向高端产业集聚，特别是党的十八大以来，高技术产业利用外资年均增长 18.4%。

Since 1998, foreign investment has continuously clustered in high-end industries. The average annual growth rate of actual use of FDI in high-tech industry since the 18th National Congress of the CPC stands at 18.4%.

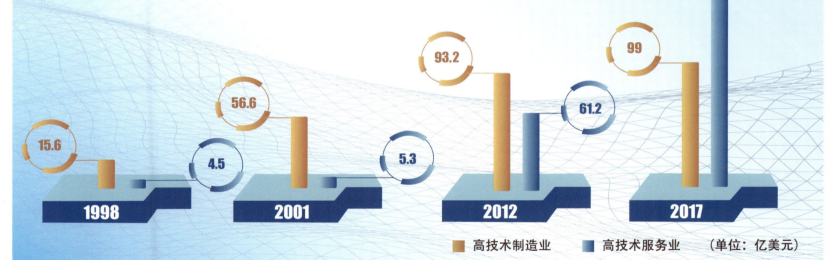

高技术制造业　　高技术服务业　　（单位：亿美元）

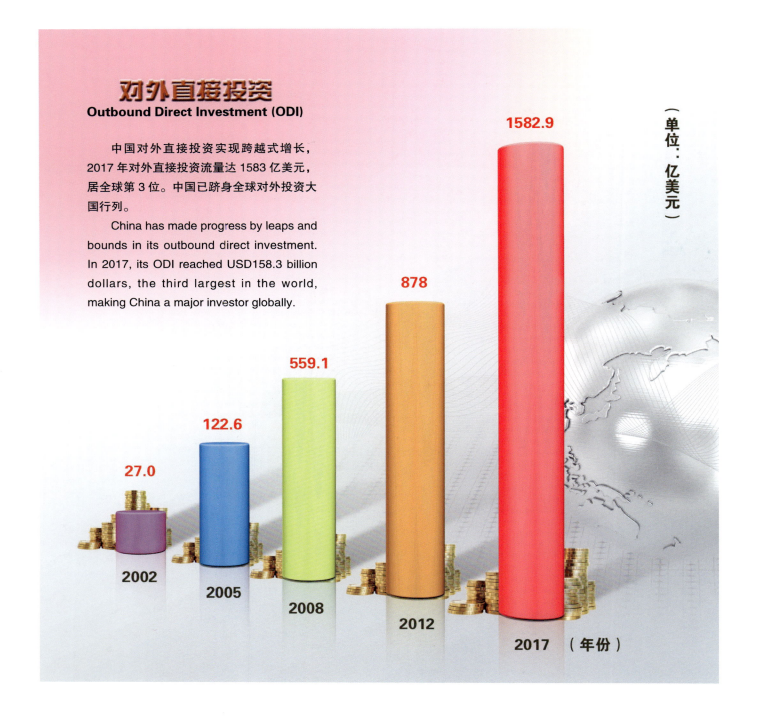

对外直接投资
Outbound Direct Investment (ODI)

中国对外直接投资实现跨越式增长，2017 年对外直接投资流量达 1583 亿美元，居全球第 3 位。中国已跻身全球对外投资大国行列。

China has made progress by leaps and bounds in its outbound direct investment. In 2017, its ODI reached USD158.3 billion dollars, the third largest in the world, making China a major investor globally.

（单位：亿美元）

1582.9

878

559.1

122.6

27.0

2002
2005
2008
2012
2017 （年份）

对外承包工程
International Project Contracting

中国对外承包工程从无到有，从小到大，已由初期土建施工加快向设计、咨询、融资等全产业链延伸。2017 年，中国对外承包工程完成营业额 1685.9 亿美元，中国已成为世界对外承包工程大国。

China's international project contracting has come a long way and expanded from civil engineering at the beginning to the whole industrial chain covering design, consulting and financing. In 2017, China's business revenue from international project contracting reached USD168.59 billion dollars. China has become a world's leading international project contractor.

（单位：亿美元）

1.0   24.0   89.0   1166.0   1685.9

1982   1992   2001   2012   2017

（年份）

对外劳务合作
International Labor Cooperation

对外劳务合作成为中国对外经济合作中不可缺少的组成部分。2017年末，中国在外劳务人数97.9万人，是1982年的近31倍。

International labor cooperation has become an integral part of China's international economic cooperation. By the end of 2017, 979,000 Chinese labors were working overseas, nearly 31 times that of 1982.

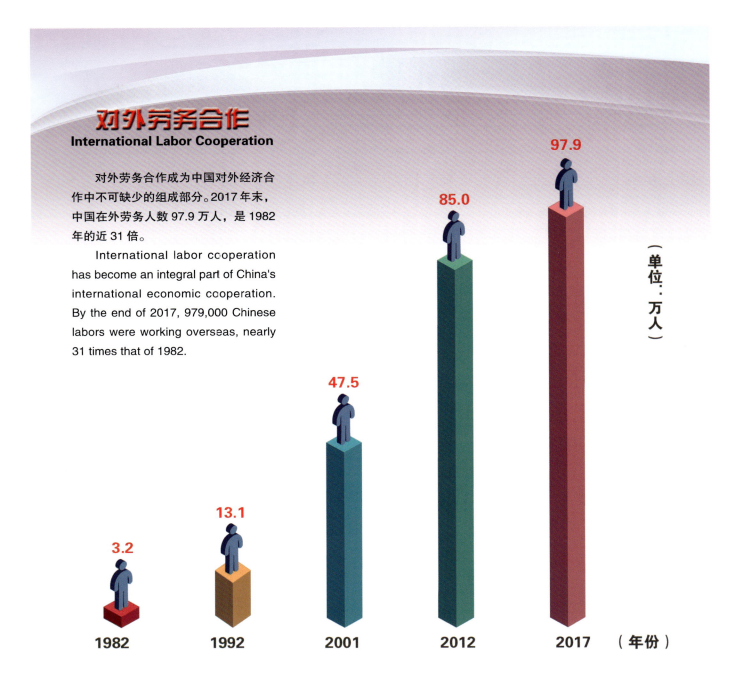

（单位：万人）

1982	1992	2001	2012	2017	（年份）
3.2	13.1	47.5	85.0	97.9	

"一带一路" 经贸合作
Trade and Economic Cooperation in the "Belt and Road" Initiative (BRI)

近年来，中国与共建国家协同努力，投资贸易规模不断扩大，合作潜力逐步释放。

In recent years, China has worked together with BRI partner countries to expand investment and trade and unleash the potential of cooperation.

（单位：亿美元）

货物进出口额   非金融类直接投资额

40 年来，中国对外贸易由小到大，目前已经成长为世界第一大货物贸易国和第二大服务贸易国，在推动中国国际化、市场化、工业化进程，促进经济社会发展，提升国际地位，扩大国际影响力等方面作出了重要贡献。

In the past 40 years, China's foreign trade grew from small to large. China has grown to the largest trader in goods and second largest trader in services in the world, making important contribution to its internationalization, marketization and industrialization, economic and social development, international prestige and influence.

第二章　贸易大国地位更加巩固
Chapter 2　An Established Big Trader

货物贸易
Trade in Goods

中国外贸持续快速发展，结构不断优化，质量效益稳步提升。

China's foreign trade continued to grow, with its structure optimized and quality and efficiency steadily improved.

❶ 进出口平衡发展
Balanced Growth of Import and Export

中国连续 9 年保持全球货物贸易第一大出口国地位。进口和出口年均增速，均快于世界以及发展中经济体年均增速。

China has maintained the world's largest exporter of goods for nine years in a row, its average annual growth rate of import and export both higher than that of the world and developing economies.

```
    |   | 2
  1 |   | 3
```

1. 2018 年 10 月，第 124 届中国进出口商品交易会（广交会）在广州琶洲会展中心开幕，来自世界各地的采购商和参展商云集。
In Oct. 2018, the 124th China Import and Export Fair (Canton fair) was opened in Guangzhou Pazhou Convention and Exhibition Center, attracting purchasers and exhibitors around the world.

2. 2018 年 11 月，首届中国国际进口博览会进博会在上海国家会展中心隆重举行。
In Nov. 2018, the first China International Import Expo (CIIE) was hosted in the National Exhibition and Convention Center (Shanghai).

3. 进博会吉祥物大熊猫"进宝"。
The mascot of the CIIE, "Jinbao".

❷ 国际市场布局更趋多元化
The Layout of International Market Has Become More Diverse

中国在巩固与传统主要贸易伙伴关系时，积极开拓与新兴经济体和发展中国家的贸易往来。

While actively strengthening trade markets with traditional key trading partners, China also actively explores trade relations with emerging economies and developing countries.

1. 2017 年 10 月，中车长春轨道客车股份有限公司研制的地铁列车成为首次登陆美国市场的国产轨道交通装备。
In Oct. 2017, the subway train developed by CRRC Changchun Railway Vehicles Co., Ltd. became the first domestic rail transport equipment to enter the US market.

2. 河北钢铁集团大力发展高附加值的冷轧产品，远销欧洲、美洲等地的 150 多个国家和地区。
The Hebei Iron and Steel Group strives to develop cold-rolled products with high added value, which are sold tc more than 150 countries and regions, including Europe and America.

1
2

1
—
2

1. 2017 年 4 月，印度南部城市海德拉巴附近的光伏电站，中国企业为该电站提供部分太阳能面板组件等产品。
In Apr. 2017, a PV power station near Hyderabad, a city in Southern India, Chinese companies offered part of solar panel module and other products for the station.

2. 自 1998 年生产出第一支基因重组人胰岛素产品以来，通化东宝药业已在俄罗斯、波兰、墨西哥、巴西等 20 多个国家进行注册认证。
In 1998, Tonghua Dongbao Pharmaceutical Co., Ltd. successfully developed the first recombinant human insulin with China's independent intellectual property rights. At present, the series of recombinant human insulin products are registered and certified in more than 20 countries, including Russia, Poland, Mexico and Brazil.

❸ **贸易商品结构日趋优化**
Structure of Trading in Goods Gradually Optimized

中国进出口商品结构不断向"优进优出"转变。出口商品的技术含量和附加值逐步增长，进口商品的效益进一步提升。

China's imports and exports are moving towards higher quality, with technical contents and added value further improved.

1 / 2

1. 中国通过义新欧班列进口西班牙葡萄酒。图为2017年9月在西班牙葡萄酒产区希加雷斯，村民们在葡萄酒节上跳起了传统舞蹈。
China imports Spanish wine through the Yiwu-Xinjiang-Europe cargo line. The picture shows traditional dance by local villagers at the Wine Festival in Cigales, a small town in Valladolid, a wine producing region in Spain, in Sep. 2017.

2. 智利成为中国第一大鲜果进口来源国。图为2018年1月，智利工人在为油桃装箱。
Chile has become China's largest import source of fresh fruits. In Jan. 2018, Chilean workers were packing nectarines.

1. 2013 年 9 月，来自新西兰、荷兰等 20 多个国家的企业参加北京国际乳制品及进口食品展。图为市民在展会上查看婴幼儿奶粉。

In Sep. 2013, companies from more than 20 countries, including New Zealand and Netherlands, attended the Beijing International Dairy Products and Imported Food Exhibition. The picture shows customers are taking a look at baby formula at the exhibition.

2. 海南口岸进口商品交易额持续增长。图为消费者在三亚免税店选购化妆品。

The trading volume of imports by Hainan port keeps growing. The picture shows consumers buying cosmetics in Sanya Duty Free Shop.

1. 2011 年 10 月，由上海外高桥造船有限公司自主研发建造的好望角型散货船"兰梅"号，系专门为美国量身定制的新船。
In Oct. 2011, the Capesize bulk carrier "LAN MAY" independently developed and built by Shanghai Waigaoqiao Shipbuilding Co., Ltd. was a new ship tailor made for the US.

2. 2016 年 1 月，北方重工集团工人在拆解出口到巴西圣保罗的盾构机。
In Jan. 2016, workers of the Northern Heavy Industries Group Co., Ltd. are dissembling a TBM exported to Sao Paulo, Brazil.

1. 中国航天凭借过硬技术和实力不断增加市场份额。图为搭载白俄罗斯通信卫星一号的长征三号乙运载火箭在等待发射。
The China Aerospace Science and Technology Corporation (CASC) keeps adding its market shares by strong technologies. The picture shows the Long March-3B rocket carrying Belarus Communications Satellite 1 waiting to be launched.

2. 中国出口商品结构实现了由初级产品向工业制成品为主的历史性转变，高新技术产品和大型成套设备占出口的比重不断提高。图为中国为巴基斯坦设计建造的第一座核电站——恰希玛核电站。
China's export mix has shifted from primary products to industrial manufactured goods. The share of new and high-tech products and large complete equipment in total export has been rising. In the picture is the first nuclear power plant designed and built by China—Chashma Nuclear Power Station in Pakistan.

作为全球第三的风电叶片制造商，江苏连云港中复连众复合材料集团产品批量出口阿根廷、英国、日本等20多个国家和地区。
As the No. 3 wind power blade manufacturer in the world, Lianyungang Zhongfu Lianzhong Composites Group Co., Ltd. located in Jiangsu Province, exports its products in batches to more than 20 countries and regions, including Argentina, the UK, Japan.

2015 年 11 月，中国自主研制的首架 C919 大型客机在上海浦东基地正式下线。
In Nov. 2015，the first C919，China's domestically designed big passenger plane in Shanghai Pudong base officially offline.

❹ 外贸动力转换不断加快
Foreign Trade Are Speeding up in Changing Its Drivers

民营企业出口比重持续增长，成为中国出口的生力军；外贸企业创新能力、品牌建设、营销能力不断增强；外贸新业态成为外贸发展的新动能、新亮点。

The share of export by private companies keeps growing, becoming a new force for China's export. The innovative abilities, brand building and marketing abilities of foreign trade enterprises keep growing and new business models become new drivers and highlights for the development of foreign trade.

1
2

1. 2016 年 1 月，小米在迪拜举行新闻发布会，全面进军中东市场。
In Jan. 2016, Xiaomi held a press conference in Dubai, announcing a general March to the Middle East market.

2. 2018 年 5 月，加拿大电信运营商发售华为 P20 系列智能手机。
In May. 2018, telecom operators in Canada started to sell Huawei Smartphones in P20 Series.

天猫国际

1
2

1. 2017 年 4 月，阿里巴巴集团杭州总部天猫国际工作区。
In Apr. 2017, workspace of Tmall.HK in the Headquarters of Alibaba in Hangzhou.

2. 跨境电商、市场采购贸易等贸易新业态蓬勃发展，成为外贸新增长点。图为跨境电商综试区内国际邮件互换站在分拣跨境电商邮包。
Cross-border e-commerce, market purchase trade and other new business models have become new growth drivers of foreign trade. The picture shows that in the Cross-border E-commerce Comprehensive Pilot Area, mails via cross-border e-commerce are being sorted at the exchange station for international mails.

❺ 与"一带一路"沿线国家货物贸易稳步发展
Steady Growth of Trade in Goods Between China and Belt and Road Countries

2014—2017 年，中国与"一带一路"相关国家货物贸易总额保持约 10000 亿美元规模。2017 年，货物贸易额达到 7.4 万亿元人民币，同比增长 17.8%。
From 2014−17, the total trade in goods between China and Belt and Road countries remained at about USD 1000 billion. In 2017, the total trade in goods was RMB 7.4 trillion, up by 17.8% year on year.

```
1
2 3
```

1. 2017 年 5 月，"一带一路"国际合作高峰论坛高级别会议"推进贸易畅通"平行主题会议在北京国家会议中心举行。
In May. 2017, the thematic session on trade connectivity under the Belt and Road Forum for International Cooperation was hosted in China National Convention Center, Beijing.

2. 2017 年 6 月，山东省沂源县玻璃制品企业的工人在检验出口印尼、俄罗斯的产品。
In Jun. 2017, the workers of glass companies in Shandong were testing products to be exported to Indonesia and Russia.

3. 2017 年 5 月，叙利亚商人在浙江义乌国际商贸城采购工艺品。
In May. 2017, Syrian merchants were purchasing artifacts in Yiwu International Trade City, Zhejiang.

1
2

1. 2017 年 4 月，瑞典客商在第三届中国（泉州）海上丝绸之路国际品牌博览会上了解中国德化白瓷。
In Apr. 2017, Swedish customers learn about Dehua white porcelain at the 3rd China (Quanzhou) Maritime Silk Road International Brand Expo.

2. "万里茶道"融入"一带一路"。图为 2017 年 4 月，武夷山茶农在采摘春茶。
The Tea Road (China) Cooperative is integrating into the Belt and Road. The picture shows Wuyishan tea farmers were picking spring tea in Apr. 2017.

加工贸易
Processing Trade

历经 40 年的探索实践，中国加工贸易政策体系日趋完善，方式和结构不断优化，经历了从无到有、从小到大、从大到优的具有中国特色的发展之路。

After 40 years of exploration and practice, China's processing trade has witnessed improved policy system, approaches and structure. It has started from scratch and emerged stronger on the development path with Chinese characteristics.

❶ 起步探索
Initial Exploration

1981 年中国加工贸易进出口额为 25 亿美元，1988 年迅速增至 287 亿美元，增长约 10 倍。

China's import and export for processing trade soared from USD2.5 billion in 1981 to USD28.7 billion in 1988, up by 10 fold.

1 | 2

1. 1978 年创办的我国首批加工贸易企业之一——广东省东莞市太平手袋厂。
Taiping Handbag Manufacturing Plant in Dongguan, Guangdong Province, one of the first processing trade enterprises set up in 1978.

2. 1988 年，广东省南海县平洲镇出产的各式男女皮鞋出口欧美和东南亚各国。图为技术人员在研究设计皮鞋。
In 1988, men and women footwear produced by Pingzhou town, Nanhai county, Guangdong province, was exported to Europe, the US, and Southeast Asia. The photo shows technicians working on the design of the shoes.

❷ 快速发展
Rapid Development

1989—2003 年，中国加工贸易进出口额由 362 亿美元大幅增加到 4048 亿美元，增长约 10 倍，年均增长 18.8%。
Between 1989 and 2003, China's import and export for processing trade surged from USD36.2 billion to USD404.8 billion, up by 10 times at an annual rate of 18.8%.

福建省莆田县江口镇发挥侨乡优势，大力发展以出口创汇为重点的电子工业。图为 1992 年女工正在检查小型游戏机的质量。
Jiangkou town, Putian county, Fujian province, hometown to many overseas Chinese, focused on electronic industry to earn foreign exchange through export. The photo shows workers checking the quality of video games.

❸ 调整转型
Adjustment and Transition

2004—2010 年，中国加工贸易进出口额由 5497 亿美元扩大到 11578 亿美元，年均增长 13.2%。

Between 2004 and 2010, China's import and export for processing trade surged from USD549.7 billion to USD1.1578 trillion, with an annual growth rate of 13.2%.

1 | 2
———
3

1. 2007 年 6 月，北海出口加工区企业工人在组装激光头。
Workers in Beihai export processing zone assembling laser heads, Jun. 2007.

2. 珠三角地区外向型企业有"世界工厂"之称。图为化妆品公司员工在实验室工作。
The export-oriented companies in the Pearl River Delta are known as the "world's factory". The photo shows staff of a cosmetic company working in the laboratory.

3. 风神轮胎股份有限公司硫化生产线。
Vulcanization production line of Fengshen Tire Co., Ltd.

❹ 升级创新
Upgrading and Innovation

2007—2010 年，为支持中西部承接加工贸易转移，商务部会同人力资源和社会保障部、海关总署共同培育认定了三批共 44 个加工贸易重点承接地。第一批包括湖南省郴州市等 9 个地区，第二批包括重庆市、河南省郑州市等 22 个地区，第三批包括辽宁省锦州市等 13 个地区。

Between 2007 and 2010, in order to support the Midwest to undertake processing trade transfer, the Ministry of Commerce in conjunction with the Ministry of Human Resources and social security, the General Administration of Customs jointly cultivated and identified three batches of a total of 44 processing trade focus. The first group included 9 regions, such as Chenzhou, Hunan province; the second group included 22 regions such as Chongqing and Zhengzhou, Henan province; the third group included 13 regions, such as Jinzhou, Liaoning province.

1

2

1. 中国东部地区劳动密集型、资源密集型产业逐步向中西部地区转移。左图为湖南省郴州出口加工区，右图为富士康科技集团 IT 零部件生产项目落户郑州出口加工区。

Labor-intensive and resource-intensive industries in eastern China are gradually moving to the central and western regions. The picture on the left shows Chenzhou Export Processing Zone in Hunan and the right shows Foxconn Technology Group, which sets up an IT component manufacturing facility in Zhengzhou Export Processing Zone.

2. 中国出口企业不断壮大，持续转型升级。图为全国加工贸易转型升级示范企业——东莞劲胜精密组件股份有限公司的自动化生产线。

Chinese exporting enterprises have gone from strength to strength and continued to transform and upgrade themselves. In the picture is the automated production line of Janus (Dongguan) Precision Components Co., Ltd, a model enterprise for transformation and upgrading of processing trade in China.

服务贸易

Trade in Service

经过 40 年的发展，中国服务贸易实现历史性跨越，已跻身世界服务贸易大国行列。

After 40 years of development, China's trade in service has made historic leaps forward and China has become a major trader in services in the world.

❶ 规模不断扩大

Expanded Size

1982—2017 年，中国服务贸易总额从 47 亿美元增至 6957 亿美元。

From 1982 to 2017, China's trade in service soared from USD4.7 billion to USD695.7 billion.

2018 年 5 月，第五届中国（北京）国际服务贸易交易会开幕，吸引了 120 个国家和地区办展参会。图为京交会举办地国家会议中心。

In May 2018, the fifth China (Beijing) International Fair for Trade in Services opened with exhibitions staged by 120 countries and regions. In the picture is the National Convention Center where CIFTIS is held.

1

2

1. 中国已经成为世界第二大服务进口国，中国市场吸收了全球服务出口的十分之一。左图为中国游客在境外旅游，右图为中国留学生在美国耶鲁大学。
China is the world's second largest importer of services. One tenth of services exported in the world go to the China market. In the pictures are Chinese tourists in foreign countries (left) and Chinese students in Yale University (right).

2. 中远海运（比雷埃夫斯）港口有限公司是中远海运集团第一家海外控股的港口有限公司。
COSCO Shipping Co., Ltd. (Piraeus) is the first foreign port company controlled by COSCO.

❷ 新兴服务贸易快速发展
Rapid Growth of Emerging Service Trade

2017 年，中国电信、计算机和信息服务，个人、文化和娱乐服务，维护和维修服务等新兴服务贸易出口达 1084.9 亿美元。

In 2017, China exported USD108.49 billion worth of emerging service, including telecommunications, computing and information service, personal, cultural and entertainment service, maintenance and repair service, etc.

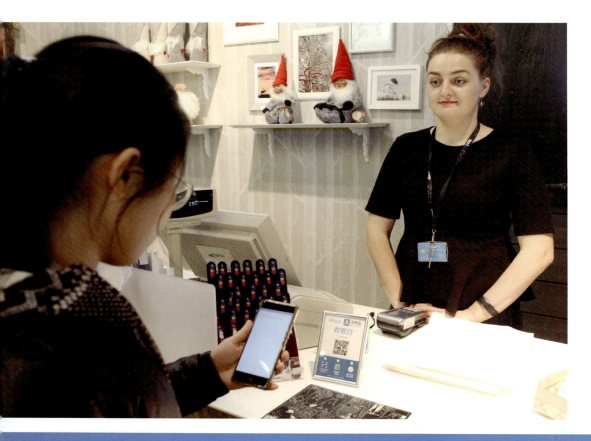

1 |

2

1. 游客在芬兰赫尔辛基使用中国移动支付平台。
Tourists use Chinese mobile payment platform in Helsinki.

2. 北京市推动文化贸易改革，创立文物艺术品"区内存储 + 区外展拍"保税交易模式。图为国家对外文化贸易基地（北京）。
Beijing endeavors to reform cultural trade by creating a bonded transaction model for cultural relics and artifacts. Those goods are stored in the bonded zone and exhibited and auctioned outside. The picture shows the National Base for International Cultural Trade (Beijing).

1 |
—
2 |

1. 2015 年，华为向苹果许可专利 769 件。图为华为公司研发人员正在测试无线产品的可靠性指标。
In 2015, Huawei authorized 769 patents to Apple. The photo shows the technicians of Huawei performing a reliability test on the wireless product.

2. 2017 年 2 月，北京通航法荷航飞机航线维修有限责任公司揭牌成立。
In Feb. 2017, AFI KLM E&M—BGAC Line Maintenance Co., Ltd was inaugurated.

❸ 广泛开展与"一带一路"沿线国家的服务贸易
Service Trade with Belt and Road Partner Countries

2017 年，中国与"一带一路"沿线国家的服务贸易额 997.6 亿美元，占当年服务贸易总额的 14.1%。
In 2017, China's service trade with Belt and Road partner countries reached USD99.76 billion, accounting for 14.1% of the total service trade of the year.

1
―――
2

1. 在俄罗斯首都莫斯科的加加林阿特拉斯宇航中心，中国游客在俄罗斯宇航员的保护之下体验太空失重训练的乐趣。
Chinese tourists experiencing zero gravity in the Gagarin Cosmonauts Training Center, Moscow, Russia.

2. 2015 年 1 月，"美丽中国·丝绸之路"旅游年启动仪式在陕西西安举行。
In Jan. 2015, the Silk Road Tourism Year launching ceremony was held in Xi'an, Shaanxi.

1
2

1. 同仁堂向国内外游客展示介绍中医药。
Tongrentang introduces traditional Chinese medicine to visitors at home and abroad.

2. 中国云服务走向"一带一路"。
Chinese cloud services in the Belt and Road initiative.

❹ 服务外包升级发展
Upgrading and Development of Service Outsourcing

2005—2017 年，服务外包业务规模从 9.33 亿美元增长至近 800 亿美元，业务结构不断优化，服务外包企业群体扩张到 4 万多家，服务外包业务占全球服务外包市场比重连续多年超过 30%。

From 2005 to 2017, the service outsourcing soared from USD933 million to USD80 billion, with improved business structure and over 40,000 players. China's service outsourcing has taken up over 30% of the global total for many years in a row.

信息技术外包转型升级步伐加快。图为携程早期的呼叫中心大厅。
IT outsourcing has sped up the pace in transformation. The photo shows a call center of Ctrip in the early days.

1
2
3

1. 知识流程外包成为主要增长引擎。图为工作人员通过平板设备展示城市博物馆 AR 体验墙。
Knowledge processing outsourcing has become a major growth engine. The photo shows a staff presenting an AR experience wall with his tablet device in a city museum.

2. 博彦科技为全球客户提供 ERP 和 BPO（业务流程外包）等服务。图为位于北京中关村软件园的博彦科技全球总部大厦。
Beyondsoft provides EPR and BPO service to global clients. The photo shows the headquarter of Beyondsoft in Beijing Zhongguancun Software Park.

3. 大连软件园是国家级软件产业基地之一，已形成软件和服务外包产业的集群效应，目前累计进驻几百家中外软件企业。
Dalian Software Park, one of the national software industrial bases, has created clustering of software and services outsourcing industries. It is home to hundreds of Chinese and foreign software firms.

1. 截至 2018 年 10 月，经国务院批准，服务外包示范城市累计达到 31 个。图为第三届中国国际服务外包合作大会在南京开幕。
By Oct. 2018, the State Council has approved 31 exemplary cities for service outsourcing. The photo shows the 3rd China International Service Outsourcing Cooperation Conference held in Nanjing.

2. 2018 年 6 月，位于济南高新区的浪潮集团高端容错计算机生产基地。
The production base for high-end fault-tolerant computer of Inspur in Jinan High-tech Industrial Development Zone, Jun. 2018.

1

2

1. 2018 年 6 月，第十六届中国国际软件和信息服务交易会在大连开幕。
In Jun. 2018, the 16th China International Software and Information Service Fair was held in Dalian.

2. 经过两年多的试验，15 个服务贸易创新发展试点地区形成了 29 条可复制可推广的政策经验。图为 2018 年 9 月，服务贸易创新发展试点和服务外包示范城市座谈会在杭州召开。
After more than two year's experiment, 15 pilot regions for innovative service trade have produced 29 replicable policies and practices. The photo shows the seminar of pilot regions for innovative service trade and exemplary cities for service outsourcing, held in Hangzhou in Sep. 2018.

第三章 利用外资水平不断提升
Chapter 3 Enhanced Foreign Direct Investment Utilization

1992 年以来，中国吸收外商投资金额一直位列发展中国家首位，在全球也名列前茅。《2017 年世界投资报告》显示，中国仍是外商投资的热土。

Since 1992, China has been the first in developing countries to absorb foreign investment, and is among the highest in the world. *The World Investment Report 2017* shows that China remains a hot destination for global investment.

吸收外资结构不断优化
Ever-improving Structure of FDI Inflows

2017 年，服务业实际使用外资总量的份额为 69.4%，制造业实际使用外资总量的份额为 24.6%。高技术产业实际利用外资增长 64.8%，其中，高技术服务业实际使用外资同比增长 106.4%，高技术制造业实际使用外资同比增长 7.6%。

In 2017, the paid-in FDI in services sector and manufacturing sector accounted for 69.4% and 24.6% of the total respectively. The actual use of FDI in high-tech industry grew by 64.8%. In breakdown, paid-in investment in high-tech services and high-tech manufacturing rose by 106.4% and 7.6% year-on-year respectively.

1. 1980 年 4 月，全国首家中外合资企业——北京航空食品有限公司成立。

In Apr. 1980, Beijing Air Catering Co., Ltd., the first Chinese-foreign joint venture was established.

1 | 2

2. 1983 年 2 月，港商投资兴建合作经营的中国第一家五星级宾馆——白天鹅宾馆正式开业。上图为白天鹅宾馆建设前的旧景，下图为白天鹅宾馆建成后的外观。

Opened in Feb. 1983, the White Swan Hotel is the first five-star hotel in China invested by a Hong Kong developer. The picture above shows the site before the construction cf the White Swan Hotel, Below is the picture of the appearance of the Hotel.

1. 1987年9月，中国第一家肯德基餐厅——北京肯德基美式炸鸡快餐厅开始试营业。
In Sep. 1987, the first KFC outlet opened in Beijing, China.

2. 1989年12月，中外合资企业中国国际贸易中心国贸大厦建成启用。
In Dec. 1989, China World Trade Center owned by a large Chinese-foreign joint venture was put into use.

1 |

2

1. 1994 年 6 月，荷兰银行上海分行在上海外滩原荷兰银行旧址开业。
In Jun. 1994, ABN AMRO opened its Shanghai branch on the old site of the Dutch bank in Waitan, Shanghai.

2. 1993 年 4 月，全国第一家中外合资大型商场——北京燕莎友谊商城成立。
In Apr. 1993, Beijing Yansha Friendship Shopping City, China's first retailing joint venture was established.

1
2

1. 2011 年 8 月，默克雪兰诺中国研发中心启用。
In Aug. 2011, Merck Serono opened its R&D center in China.

2. 1998 年进入中国市场的宜家家居。
IKEA entered the China market in 1998.

海南省三亚市鸿洲国际游艇会和意大利托斯卡纳大区的联合企业成立合资公司，在三亚打造"超级游艇"服务基地。
The joint venture established by Hongzhou International Yacht Club and an Italian Toscana company builds a super yacht service base in Sanya, Hainan.

1

2

1. 2016 年 3 月，来自台湾的青年医师（左）在平潭（台湾）爱维口腔医院为助理讲解手术方案。
In Mar. 2016, a dentist from Taiwan (left) explained surgery procedures to assistants in Pingtan (Taiwan) Aiwei Stomatological Hospital.

2. 2016 年 6 月，上海迪士尼度假区正式开园。
In Jun. 2016, Shanghai Disney Resort opened.

1. 1984 年，北京吉普汽车有限公司是中美合资经营的一家大型企业。
In 1984, Beijing Jeep, a large Sino-US joint venture, was established.

2. 1988 年，中英合资企业——上海耀华皮尔金顿玻璃有限公司正式投产。图为双方技术人员在工作中。
Shanghai Yaohua Pilkington Glass Group Co., Ltd., a Sino-UK joint venture, was put into production in 1988. The picture shows the technicians from both sides at work.

1. 1991 年，中德合资上海大众汽车有限公司作为上海最大的中外合资企业，当年生产桑塔纳轿车 35200 辆。
In 1991, Shanghai Volkswagen, a joint venture established by China and Germany and the largest Sino-foreign joint venture in Shanghai, manufactured 35,200 vehicles.

1	
2	3

2. 1997 年 10 月，西门子中国公司举行在中国安家 125 周年庆典。图为西门子公司负责人与老员工切蛋糕。
In Oct.1997, Siemens Ltd., China held its 125th anniversary celebration in China. The Photo shows the head of Siemens cut the cake with an old employee.

3. 1993 年，中荷合资企业——上海飞利浦半导体公司投产。
Philips Semiconductor Corporation of Shanghai, a Sino-Dutch joint venture, was put into production in 1993.

2016 年 3 月，空中客车天津 A330 宽体机完成和交付中心开工仪式在天津滨海新区举行。
The ground–breaking ceremony of Airbus A330 Completion and Delivery Centre (C&DC) was held in Tianjin Binhai New Area in Mar. 2016.

2017 年 10 月，美国特斯拉北京科技创新中心注册成立。图为特斯拉 Model X 电动汽车。
The Tesla Beijing Technology Innovation Center was registered in Oct. 2017. In the picture is Tesla Model X.

吸收外资区域布局不断优化
Ever–improving Geographical Distribution of FDI

中国东部利用外资依然占据主导地位。为促进外商投资的区域平衡发展，国家出台了《关于支持沿边重点地区开发开放若干政策措施的意见》，4 次修订《中西部地区外商投资优势产业目录》，总条目达到639 条，以增强中西部、东北和沿边地区对外商投资的吸引力。

East China remains the favorite destination for foreign investment coming in the country. In order to ensure FDI regional balance, China issued the *Opinions on Policies and Measure of Supporting Development and Opening Up of Priority Border Areas* (Guofa [2015] No.72) and revised the *Catalogue for the Guidance of Foreign Investment in Competitive Industries in Central and Western China* 4 times, bring the entry items up to 639 to make central and western China as well as the border areas more attractive to foreign investment.

2006 年 2 月，位于广东省惠州市大亚湾经济技术开发区内的中海壳牌南海石化项目成功投产。上图为生产基地外观。下图为中海壳牌生产基地夜景。
In Feb. 2006, CNOOC and Shell Petrochemical Co., Ltd. was put into production in Daya Bay Economic & Technological Development Zone, Huizhou, Guangdong. The pictures are appearance of the production bases.

❶ 东部地区利用外资占主体地位
FDI Utilization Concentrated in Eastern China

截至 2017 年，中国外商投资在东部、中部、西部地区的比重分别为 85.4%、7.9%、6.7%。

By 2017, eastern, central and western China had received 85.4%、7.9%、6.7% of the total FDI.

1
2

1. 2016 年 5 月，通富微电通过与 AMD 合资合作，技术达到世界一流水平。图为通富超威苏州工厂测试车间。
In May. 2016, TongFu Microelectronics developed world-class technology through its cooperation and joint venture with AMD. Above is a picture of a commissioning shop of TF-AMD's factory in Suzhou.

2. 中意合资山东常林道依茨法尔机械有限公司技术人员在装配车间内交流。
Technicians of Shandong Changlin-DeutzFahr, a Sino-Italian joint venture, are communicating in an assembly shop.

❷ 中西部地区对外商投资吸引力逐步增强
Central and Western Region's Ever-increasing Appeal towards Foreign Investors
中国出台相关政策，以增强中西部、东北和沿边地区对外商投资的吸引力。
China adopted relevant policies to enhance the appeal of its central and western region as well as border areas towards foreign investors.

1 |
2

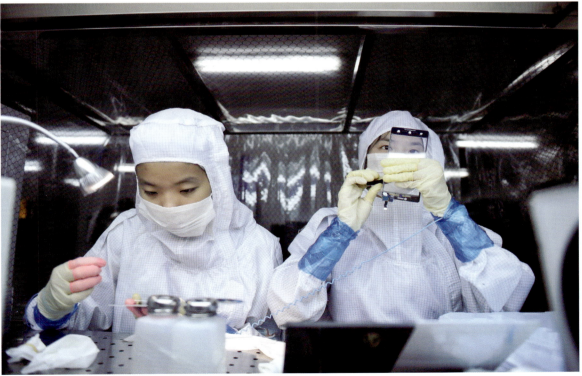

1. 长沙经济技术开发区内外资企业德国博世汽车生产车间。
Vehicle manufacturing shop of Bosch, a German enterprise in Changsha Economic and Technological Development Zone.

2. 2014 年 11 月，江西联创电子与韩国美法思株式会社合资设立江西联思触控技术有限公司。图为工人在生产智能手机触摸屏。
In Nov. 2014, Jiangxi LCE and South Korean company Melfas set up a joint venture, Jiangxi MLC. The picture shows workers producing touch screens for smart phones.

1
—
2

1. 2007 年 7 月，由沙特阿拉伯投资的新疆爱立泽纺织有限公司成立。图为沙特驻华使节参观该公司。
In Jul. 2007, Saudi-invested Xinjiang Alzeeh Textile Co., Ltd was set up. The picture shows Saudi diplomatic envoys to china visiting the company.

2. 韩泰轮胎重庆工厂的现代化生产厂房。
Modern manufacturing shop of Hankook Tire's factory in Chongqing.

1
2

1. 2012 年 9 月，由外商独立投资和开发的敦煌 18 兆瓦光伏并网发电项目建成投产。
In Sep. 2012, the 18-magewatt grid-connected photovoltaic power generation project in Dunhuang invested and developed solely by foreign investors came into operation.

2. 2013 年 10 月，由山西太钢集团和美国哈斯科公司共同投资建设的钢渣综合利用项目进入试生产阶段。图为工人在对生产出来的专用化肥进行包装。
In Oct. 2013, the steel slag comprehensive utilization project invested and constructed by Shanxi Tisco and US company Harscowent into commissioning. The picture shows workers packing special-utility fertilizer.

营商环境持续改善
Business Climate Keeps Improving

2018 年 6 月，国务院发布《关于积极有效利用外资推动经济高质量发展若干措施的通知》（国发〔2018〕19 号），从投资自由化、投资便利化、投资促进、投资保护、优化区域开放布局、推动国家级开发区创新六个方面提出具体优化措施。世界银行发布的《2019 营商环境报告》显示，中国营商环境全球排名从第 78 位跃升至第 46 位。

In Jun. 2018, the State Council released the *Notice on Certain Measures for Actively and Effectively Utilizing Foreign Investment to Promote Quality Economic Development* (Guofa [2018] No.19), setting out specific measures for investment liberalization and facilitation, investment promotion and protection, optimized architecture for regional opening-up, and innovation promotion in national development zones. According to the *Doing Business 2019 report* of the World Bank, China has climbed from the 78th place to the 46th place in the world in the business environment ranking.

❶ 放宽投资准入
Easing Market Access

2018 年 6 月，经党中央、国务院同意，国家发展改革委、商务部发布《外商投资准入特别管理措施（负面清单）》（2018 年版）《自由贸易试验区外商投资准入特别管理措施（负面清单）》（2018 年版）。全国版负面清单进一步缩减到 48 项，自贸试验区的负面清单进一步在文化、资源、种业、电信等领域进行开放的压力测试。

In June 2018, at the approval of the CPC Central Committee and the State Council, the National Development and Reform Commission and the Ministry of Commerce released the *Special Administrative Measures on Foreign Investment* (Negative List)(2018) and the *Special Administrative Measures on Foreign Investment Access to Pilot Free Trade Zones* (Negative List) (2018). The nationwide negative list was shortened to 48 entries, while the negative list for the PFTZs had further stress tests for the opening-up of the cultural, resources, seeding, and telecoms sector.

中华人民共和国国家发展和改革委员会
中华人民共和国商务部 令

第 18 号

《外商投资准入特别管理措施（负面清单）（2018 年版）》已经党中央、国务院同意，现予以发布，自 2018 年 7 月 28 日起施行。2017 年 6 月 28 日国家发展和改革委员会、商务部发布的《外商投资产业指导目录（2017 年修订）》中的外商投资准入特别管理措施（外商投资准入负面清单）同时废止，鼓励外商投资产业目录继续执行。

国家发展和改革委员会主任：何立峰

商务部部长：钟山

2018 年 6 月 28 日
— 1 —

中华人民共和国国家发展和改革委员会
中华人民共和国商务部 令

第 19 号

《自由贸易试验区外商投资准入特别管理措施（负面清单）（2018 年版）》已经党中央、国务院同意，现予以发布，自 2018 年 7 月 30 日起施行。2017 年 6 月 5 日国务院办公厅印发的《自由贸易试验区外商投资准入特别管理措施（负面清单）（2017 年版）》同时废止。

国家发展和改革委员会主任：何立峰

商务部部长：钟山

2018 年 6 月 30 日
— 1 —

❷ 提供便利的政务环境

Providing Convenient Government Services

商务部会同市场监管总局，于 2018 年 6 月 30 日在全国推行外商投资企业的商务备案与工商登记"一口受理"，进一步节约企业成本，优化政府服务。

The Ministry of Commerce and the State Administration for Market Regulation rolled out the "single window" for the record-filing and business registration across the country for foreign-invested companies starting from June 30, 2018, in an effort to save business cost and improve government services.

1	2
	3

1. 商务部业务系统统一平台界面。
User interface of the integrated business platform of the Ministry of Commerce.

2. 2017 年 4 月，北京市外资企业备案与登记"单一窗口、单一表格"正式启动。
In Apr. 2017, the Beijing Municipal government officially launched the "single window, single form" for the record-filing and business registration of foreign-invested companies.

3. 广东自贸试验区南沙片区综合服务大厅为申请人提供企业设立登记"一口受理"服务。图为工作人员为企业和个人提供企业设立登记的咨询、指导和申请材料帮核服务。
The comprehensive services hall of China (Guangdong) Pilot Free Trade Zone Nansha Area provides applicants with company establishment and registration services through a "single window". The picture shows a staff member providing enterprises and individuals with consultancy, guidance and documents checking services related to company establishment and registration.

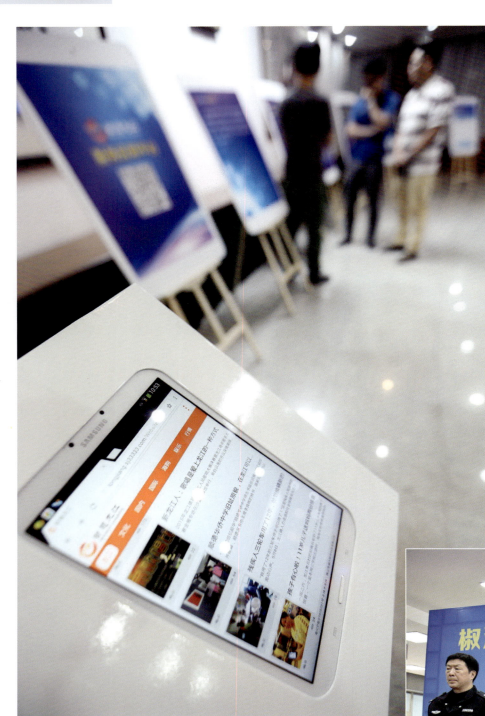

1
2

1. 2015 年 5 月开通的佛山顺德"智慧龙江"公共服务平台，为政府提高公共服务水平、优化投资环境提供了强有力的支持。图为市民在观看平台应用展板。
The public service platform of Foshan Shunde "Smart Longjiang", which opened in May. 2015, provides strong support for the Government to improve the level of public service and optimize the investment environment. The picture shows citizens looking at boards.

2. 自 2017 年 1 月起，浙江省台州市椒江区在全省首推"九证合一"登记制度改革。
In Jan. 2017, Jiaojiang district, Taizhou, Zhejiang province, became the first in Zhejiang to reform its registration system and merge nine different forms of certification required of businesses into one certificate.

❸ 增强权益保护
Strengthening Rights Protection
积极保护外商在华知识产权等权益。
Actively protecting foreign investors' IPR and other rights and interests in China.

1	2
	3

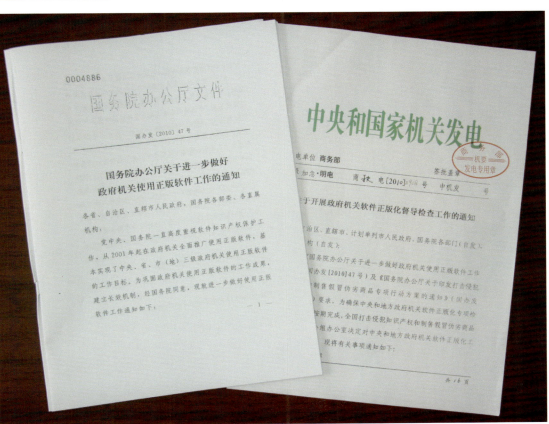

1. "12312"已成为公众所熟知的知识产权举报投诉电话。图为外国使节参观北京保护知识产权举报投诉服务中心。
"12312", the IPR infringement report hotline, has become a well-known phone number among the public. Above is a picture of foreign envoys visiting the Beijing Service Center for Intellectual Property Protection.

2. 2016年7月，来自约旦的外商在浙江省义乌市获得了"义乌国际卡"，将享受基本养老、子女教育等保障。
In Jul. 2016, a Jordanian investor got his "Yiwu International Card" in Yiwu, Zhejiang province, which means he gained access to services like basic old-age care and education for his children.

3. 2010年12月，商务部下发《关于开展政府机关软件正版化督导检查工作的通知》。
In Dec. 2010, MOFCOM issued the *Circular on Supervision and Inspection of Authorized Software Installation in Government Bodies.*

开发区吸收外资升级转型

Upgrading and Transformation of Development Zones through FDI Utilization

东部沿海国家级经开区开放创新、优化资源配置，中西部地区和东北老工业基地国家级经开区积极推进发展，取得明显效益。

Along the east coast, national economic development zones optimize resource allocation through opening–up and innovation; in the central and western region and old industrial bases in the northeast, development zones have made remarkable progress in promoting development.

```
          1
      ┌──────
  2   │
```

1. 早期天津经济技术开发区。
Tianjin Economic–Technological Development Area in the past.

2. 2018年，天津经济技术开发区成为中国经济规模最大、外向型程度最高、综合投资环境最优的国家级开发区之一。
In 2018, Tianjin Economic–Technological Development Area became one of China's most trade–oriented national development zones with the largest economic output and best overall investment climate.

苏州工业园是中国与新加坡两国政府间重要的合作项目，1994年经国务院批准设立的国家级经济技术开发区。图为1995年和2018年苏州工业园区金鸡湖李公堤开发前后。Suzhou Industrial Park is an important inter-governmental cooperation project between China and Singapore. It is a national economic and technology development zone approved by the State Council in 1994. The photo shows the Jinji Lake and Ligong Levee of the park in 1995 and 2018, before and after the development of the project.

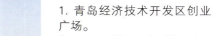

1. 青岛经济技术开发区创业广场。
Start-up Plaza in Qingdao Economic and Technological Development Zone.

2. 自1993年建区以来，西安经济技术开发区已初步发展成为一个外向型的现代工业园区和城市新区。图为西安经济技术开发区。
Since its establishment in 1993, Xi'an Economic and Technological Development Zone has developed into a trade-oriented modern industrial park and urban district. The picture shows a view of the development zone.

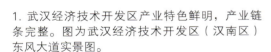

1. 武汉经济技术开发区产业特色鲜明，产业链条完整。图为武汉经济技术开发区（汉南区）东风大道实景图。
Wuhan Economic and Technological Development Zone has developed distinctive sectors and complete industrial chains. The picture shows Dongfeng Avenue in Wuhan Economic and Technological Development Zone (Hannan area).

2. 长沙经济技术开发区突出主业，致力打造"中国力量之都"，全力建设现代化生态工业新城，发挥园区在区域经济中的示范和辐射带动作用。图为长沙经济技术开发区夜景。
Changsha Economic and Technological Development Zone has a strong focus in its development. It aims at building "China's engine", building a new, modern, ecological and industrial city as well as developing its demonstration and radiation effect in driving regional economic development. The picture shows the night view of the zone.

中国积极主动参与国际分工，利用好两种资源两个市场，高水平、高质量的走出去国际经济合作格局正在形成。

An active player in the international division of labor, China is making the best use of both domestic and international resources and markets. High-level and high-quality outbound international economic cooperation between China and other countries is emerging.

第四章　国际经济合作不断深化
Chapter 4　Deepening International Economic Cooperation

对外直接投资
Outbound Direct Investment (ODI)

截至 2017 年末，中国对外直接投资存量 1.8 万亿美元，占全球外国直接投资流出存量的 5.9%，存量规模排名已跃升至全球第 2 位。

At the end of 2017, the stock of China's outbound direct investment reached USD 1.8 trillion dollars, accounting for 5.9% of the world total and the second largest in the world.

❶ 跨境并购日渐活跃
Active Cross-Border Mergers and Acquisitions

中国企业跨国并购不断增大，绿地项目稳步推进。2017 年完成跨国并购 431 起。

The number of cross-border M&A by Chinese companies is growing and Chinese companies are making green field investments as well. In 2017, Chinese companies cut 431 deals of cross-border M&A.

```
1 | 2
```

1. 2004 年 12 月，联想收购 IBM 个人电脑业务。
In Dec. 2004, Lenovo purchased the personal computer business of IBM.

2. 2010 年 3 月，中国吉利汽车集团收购瑞典沃尔沃轿车公司。
In Mar. 2010, Geely acquired Volvo Car Corporation of Sweden.

1. 2016 年 8 月，北京汽车集团与南非工业发展公司合资成立北汽南非汽车制造有限公司。
In Aug. 2016, the SOD turning ceremony of BAIC Automobile SA was held for the joint venture between Beijing Automotive Industry Holding Co., Ltd. and Industrial Development Corporation of South Africa.

2. 2015 年 9 月，中国中车股份有限公司在美国马萨诸塞州制造基地举行奠基仪式。
In Sep. 2015, CRRC held a ground-breaking ceremony for its manufacturing base in Massachusetts, the United States.

❷ 民营企业发挥越来越大作用
The Growing Role of Private Chinese Businesses

民营企业对外投资快速发展，投资占比逐年持续增长。

Outbound investment by private Chinese companies is increasing rapidly, accounting for a growing share in China's total outbound investment.

1

2

1. 中国民营企业已在非洲找到一方广阔天地，成为中国和非洲双赢发展的重要推动力。图为位于赞比亚卢萨卡的华为公司。

Private Chinese companies have established presence in the vast African continent and become important drivers of win-win development between China and Africa. This picture shows Huawei's subsidiary in Lusaka, Zambia.

2. 福耀玻璃集团 2014 年收购美国俄亥俄州莫雷恩的闲置厂房建设汽车玻璃制造工厂。图为中国福耀玻璃集团莫雷恩工厂车间。

In 2014, Fuyao Glass bought idle workshops in Moraine, Ohio and turned them into manufacturing facilities for automotive glass in the United States. This picture shows a Fuyao Glass workshop in Moraine.

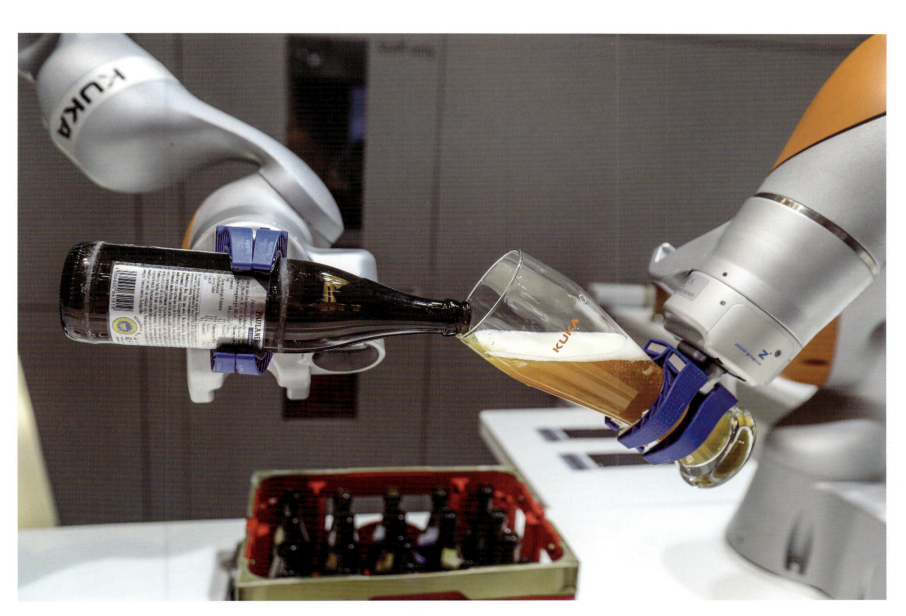

2017 年 1 月，美的集团完成对于库卡机器人（KUKA）94.55% 股份的收购。图为库卡公司在德国汉诺威工业博览会上展示两条机械臂倒啤酒。
In Jan. 2017, Midea formally concluded its purchase of 94.55% stakes of KUKA Robotics. This picture shows a KUKA robot pouring beer in Hannover Fair.

❸ **投资地域多元化**
Diverse Investment Destinations

中国对外直接投资的投资目的地日益多样化。
The investment destinations for China's OFDI are becoming increasingly diversified.

1 |
2

1. 2017 年 4 月，海尔巴基斯坦工厂负责人在笔记本电脑生产区调研。
In Apr. 2017, an executive in Haier Pakistan inspected laptop computer production.

2. 中国海信集团建立的海信南非工业园。
Hisense South Africa Industrial Park established by China Hisense Group.

1	2
3	

1. 巴基斯坦卡拉奇核电站 K2、K3 机组项目是中国具有自主知识产权的百万千瓦级核电技术"华龙一号"机组的首次出口。图为 K2 号机组核岛穹顶吊装现场。
The Karachi K2 and K3 nuclear plants are the first time for China's proprietary nuclear technology, Hualong One, with million kilowatt power, to be exported. The photo shows the installation of the nuclear island of the K2 unit.

2. 沙特阿拉伯延布炼油厂项目由中国石化与沙特阿美公司共同投资建设，总投资约 86 亿美元。
The Yanbu refinery project in Saudi Arabia was co-invested by Sinopec and Aramco, with a total investment of USD8.6 billion.

3. 奇瑞汽车股份有限公司建立的奇瑞巴西汽车工业园。
The Auto Industry Park in Brazil of Chery Automobile Co., Ltd.

❹ 境外经贸合作区成为"走出去"的重要载体
Overseas Economic and Trade Cooperation Zones as Important Platforms in Outbound Investment

截至 2017 年底，中国企业已建成初具规模的境外经贸合作区 99 家，分布在 44 个国家，累计投资 307 亿美元，入区企业 4364 家，成为国际产能合作的重要载体和平台。

By the end of 2017, Chinese companies had established 99 sizable overseas economic and trade cooperation zones in 44 countries, with total investment of USD30.7 billion dollars. As many as 4,364 businesses had established presence in these zones, making them important vehicles and platforms in international production capacity cooperation.

1	
2	

1. 位于越南的龙江工业园。
Longjiang Industrial Park in Vietnam.

2. 招商局集团参与兴建的中白工业园。左图为中白工业园入口处的"巨石"标志，右图为中白工业园夜景。
China Merchants Group participated in the building of China–Belarus Great Stone Industrial Park. The picture on the left shows the Great Stone symbol at the entrance of the industrial park and the picture on the right shows the scene of the park at night.

1
___
2

1. 位于埃及的中埃·泰达苏伊士经
贸合作区。
China-Egypt TEDA Suez Economic
and Trade Cooperation Zone in
Egypt.

2. 位于匈牙利的中匈宝思德经贸合
作区。
China-Hungary Borsod Economic
and Trade Cooperation Zone in
Hungary.

对外承包工程
International Project Contracting

对外承包工程业务历经 40 年，从 1979 年新签合同额仅 0.33 亿美元，发展壮大到 2017 年的 2652.8 亿美元。从事对外承包工程的中国企业数量从初期的不足 30 家，增长到 2017 年底的近 5000 家。

China's international project contracting has come a long way in the past four decades, from USD33 million worth of new contracts signed in 1979 to USD265.28 billion dollars in 2017. The number of involved Chinese businesses increased from less than 30 at the beginning to nearly 5,000 at the end of 2017.

❶ 政策监管体系日趋完善
Improving Policy and Regulatory System

2017 年，取消了对外承包工程资格审批，将对外承包工程项目由投（议）标核准改为备案管理，提高了行政效率。

In 2017, the Chinese government revoked the approval procedure on the qualification for international project contracting bidding/tender and replaced it with a record filing process to increase administrative efficiency.

❷ 业务模式推陈出新
New Business Models

商务部提出基础设施合作建营一体化发展方向，鼓励企业承揽特许经营类工程项目（包括 BOT、BOO、PPP 模式等）。

MOFCOM promoted infrastructure international cooperation that integrates construction and operation and encouraged Chinese companies to undertake franchising engineering projects, including BOT, BOO and PPP models.

	2
1	

1. 中远海运控股并经营的希腊比雷埃夫斯港，已成为 21 世纪海上丝绸之路通往中东欧的门户。
Piraeus Port of Greek, which is controlled and operated by Chinese companies, has become a gateway of the 21st Century Maritime Silk Road to Central and Eastern Europe.

2. 老挝南立 1−2 水电站是三峡集团第一个 BOOT 投资项目，获 2015 年度国家优质投资项目奖。
Nam Khan 1−2 hydro power station in Laos, the first BOOT investment project of Three Gorges Group, won National Investment Project Award in 2015.

1. 2016 年 9 月，中国东方电气集团有限公司采取 BOT 模式建设的波黑斯坦纳瑞火电站项目竣工投产。
In Sep. 2016, the Stanari Coal-fired Thermal Power Plant in Bosnia and Herzegovina, built by China Dongfang Electric Corporation under a BOT mode, went into operation.

2. 2018 年 5 月，中油工程伊拉克格拉芙油田水管理系统 EPCC 项目施工现场。
The construction site of Garraf oilfield water management system EPCC project undertaken by China Petroleum Engineering and Construction Group in Iraq in May. 2018.

❸ 业务领域不断升级
Upgrading Business Scope

中国对外承包工程业务领域不断向技术含量较高的通信工程、核能和平利用、化工等方向优化升级。
Chinese companies have upgraded and expanded their international project contracting into technologically intensive areas such as telecom, civilian nuclear, petrochemical and other sectors.

1

2

1. 2009 年，由中国通信建设集团有限公司承建的坦桑尼亚国家 ICT（信息与通讯技术）宽带骨干网项目开始实施。图为 ICT 宽带骨干网项目互联网数据中心。
In 2009, China International Telecommunication Construction Corporation started to build National ICT Broadband Backbone project in Tanzania. This picture shows the Internet data center of the project.

2. 2017 年 8 月，中国企业参股投资的英国欣克利角 C 核电项目正加紧建设。
In Aug. 2017, the construction of Hinkley Point C nuclear power station invested and partly owned by a Chinese company was in full swing.

由中国机械进出口（集团）有限公司和中国五环工程有限公司联合承建的越南金瓯氮肥厂。
The Ca Mau fertilizer factory in Viet Nam, jointly undertaken by China National Machinery Import and Export Corp. and Wuhuan Engineering Co., Ltd.

④ **业务市场多元化**
Business and Market Diversification

2017 年，中国开展承包工程业务的国家（地区）已达 196 个。
In 2017, China's contractual engineering footprint covered 196 countries (regions).

上海建工集团承建的柬埔寨达克茂巴萨河大桥。
The bridge across Tonle Bassac River of Cambodia built by Shanghai Construction (Group) General Company.

中国港湾工程有限公司承建的马来西亚槟城第二跨海大桥。
The Second Penang Bridge of Malaysia built by China Harbour.

中国葛洲坝集团公司承建的埃塞俄比亚特克泽大坝。
Tekeze Dam of Ethiopia built by China Gezhouba Group Corporation.

对外劳务合作
Overseas Labor Cooperation

中国对外劳务合作事业取得了重要成就，2017 年末在外劳务人数 97.9 万人。

China's overseas labor cooperation has scored remarkable results; 979 thousand Chinese labors were working overseas by the end of 2017.

❶ 市场多元化发展
Market Diversification

中国对外劳务合作业务形成"亚洲为主、非洲为辅、欧洲和拉美稳步推进、北美和大洋洲取得进展"的市场格局。

China's overseas labor cooperation has forged a landscape of Asia as base and Africa as complement with steady advances in Europe and Latin America and progress in North America and Oceania.

1│
2│

1. 在合肥跨国劳务输出人员培训中心，农民工参加技能培训。
Migrant workers on a skill training program at Hefei Overseas labor Training Center.

2. 2014 年 8 月，河南省滑县出入境管理人员为前往印度尼西亚工作的农民工集中办理护照。
In Aug.2014, in Huaxian County, Henan Province, Exit-entry Administration officers concentrated on passports for peasant workers who went to work in Indonesia.

❷ 部分行业已形成竞争优势
Sectoral Competitive Advantages

建筑业、制造业和交通运输业已成为中国对外劳务合作的三大传统领域，三大行业的劳务人员之和约占在外总人数的 3/4 。

Construction, manufacturing and transportation are the three established areas for China's overseas labor cooperation, accounting for 3/4 of the total labor overseas when combined.

1
—
2

1. 湖北外派海员出行前集训。
Sailors from Hubei Province receiving pre-dispatch training.

2. 建筑工人集体前往以色列务工。
Construction workers collectively went to work in Israel.

1. 大连企业承建的苏里南道路工程受到苏里南政府的高度评价。图为苏里南总统与大连国际合作公司员工合影。
Roads in Suriname built by a Dalian company are highly praised by the government of Suriname. The picture shows the President of Suriname with staff of Dalian International Cooperation Corporation.

2. 参加印度尼西亚北苏门答腊省一座电站建设的中国工人。
Chinese workers building a power plant in North Sumatra, Indonesia.

❸ 对外劳务合作助力精准扶贫
Overseas Labor Cooperation Supports Precision Poverty Alleviation

商务部选择 100 家大型对外劳务合作企业与国家级贫困县结对帮扶，指导地方利用各种资源对试点企业招收贫困地区外派劳务人员予以支持。

MOFCOM has selected 100 large overseas labor cooperation companies to pair up with national poor counties and guide localities to use resources available to support recruitment of overseas labor from poor areas.

1

2

1. 湖南省对外劳务扶贫对接会议签约现场。
A signing meeting for overseas labor to poverty alleviation in Hunan Province.

2. 青海贫困互助县出国务工扶贫项目培训现场。
A training session for overseas labor from poor counties in Qinghai Province as part of poverty relief efforts.

1. 湖南赴日护理技能实习生现场面试会。
Interviews of Japan-bound trainees of nursing skills from Hunan Province.

2. 江苏中澜公司从云南贫困地区招募工人赴日本，从事汽车零部件专业技术岗位工作。
Zhonglan Corporation of Jiangsu Province recruits workers from poor areas of Yunnan Province for auto parts technical jobs in Japan.

"一带一路" 国际合作
Belt and Road International Cooperation

2014 年以来，在多项政策措施的积极鼓励下，中国企业开展国际产能合作意愿强烈，多个重点项目持续推进，有力支持了 "一带一路" 建设。

Since 2014, encouraged by multiple policy measures, Chinese companies have been very keen to engage in international capacity cooperation, with several key projects moving ahead as strong support for Belt and Road development.

❶ 加速推进设施联通项目落地生根
Accelerating the Landing of Connectivity Projects

中国企业推动铁路、港口、管道等基础设施竣工投入使用。

Chinese companies pushed for the completion and launch of railways, ports and pipelines, among other infrastructure projects.

2017 年 5 月，完全采用中国技术、中国标准的肯尼亚蒙内铁路全线开通。图为列车从蒙内铁路沿线的马泽拉斯铁路大桥上驶过。

In May 2017, the Mombasa–Nairobi Railway that adopted Chinese technologies and standards was opened. The photo shows the train running on the Mazeras railway bridge.

2018 年 1 月，中国中铁二局集团和中国土木工程集团联合承建运营的埃塞俄比亚亚吉铁路正式投入商业运营。图为当地民众步入亚吉铁路车站。

In Jan. 2018, the Addis Ababa–Djibouti Railway jointly undertaken by China Railway No.2 Group and China Civil Engineering Construction Corporation was officially launched for commercial service. The picture shows local people walking into the train station.

中欧班列国内开行城市已达 53 个，可达欧洲 15 个国家的 45 个城市，现已累计开行超过 10000 列。图为 2017 年 10 月迪卡侬选择中国武汉作为起点驶向法国物流重镇杜尔日的企业专列发车启动，这是首个由零售企业定制的中欧班列。

The China Europe Freight Train connects 53 Chinese cities with 45 cities in 15 European countries, clocking up over 10,000 services so far. The picture shows the block train of Decathlon leaving the station at the Chinese city of Wuhan for the logistics hub Dourges in France. This is the first China–Europe Railway Express customized for a retail company.

中巴经济走廊是中国与巴基斯坦友好历史上的一个重要的里程碑，瓜达尔港已成为中巴经济走廊上的一颗璀璨明珠。
The China-Pakistan Economic Corridor is a critical milestone in the history of China-Pakistan friendship. Gwadar Port has become a shining pearl along the Corridor.

❷ 积极参与国际产能合作
Active Participation in International Capacity Cooperation
中国企业全面参与当地钢铁、石化、电力等行业的产能合作。
Chinese companies are fully engaged in local capacity cooperation in steel, petrochemicals and electricity, among others.

1 | 1. 2016 年 4 月，中国河钢集团与塞尔维亚政府签约，以
4600 万欧元收购斯梅代雷沃钢铁厂。图为钢铁厂一角。
In Apr. 2016, HBIS Group signed an agreement with
the Serbian government to acquire Smederevo Steel
Company, shown in the picture above, for 46 million euro.

2 | 2. 2015 年 8 月，中石化中原油田员工与沙特阿美石油公司
员工在沙特东部一油田钻井平台前合影。
In Aug. 2015, staff of Zhongyuan Oilfield, Sinopec posed
for a photo with Aramco employees in front of an oil rig in
the east of Saudi Arabia.

1
2

1. 2018 年 8 月，中国国家电投积极响应"一带一路"倡议，在智利投资建设首个风电场——蓬塔谢拉风电场。
In Aug. 2018, the State Power Investment Corporation, in warm response to the Belt and Road initiative, invested in and built the Punta Sierra wind farm , Chile's first wind farm.

2. 2018 年 9 月，中巴经济走廊首个水电投资项目卡洛特水电站顺利实现大江截流。
In Sep. 2018, river closure was completed for Karot Hydropower Station, the first hydropower project of China–Pakistan Economic Corridor.

2018 年 8 月，由中国电建所属山东电建三公司总承包的摩洛哥
努奥光热电站三期项目发电机首次并网成功。
In Aug. 2018, generators of NOOR III Concentrated Solar
Power (CSP) project in Morocco undertaken by Sepco III under
Power China were successfully connected to grid.

改革开放以来，中国对外援助不断拓展深化，在基础设施、农业减贫、医疗卫生、生态环保、人道主义援助、能力建设等领域全面发力，形成了全方位、多层次、内容丰富的对外援助体系，充分发挥了对外援助的综合效益。

Since the reform and opening-up, China has expanded and deepened foreign assistance across the board: infrastructure, agriculture, poverty reduction, healthcare, ecological preservation, humanitarian assistance, and capacity building, putting in place an all-dimensional, multi-tiered, and enriched foreign assistance system that has delivered comprehensive benefits.

第五章 中国对外援助成效突出

Chapter 5 China's Outstanding Contribution to Effective Foreign Assistance

创新援助方式

Innovative Approaches to Foreign Assistance

从传统的无偿援助、无息贷款及优惠贷款，发展到设立"南南合作援助基金"等。

The funding China provides has evolved from grant, interest free loans and concessional loans to the establishment of South−South Cooperation Fund, etc.

1

2

1. 津巴布韦哈拉雷郊区的警署家属区装上中国提供无息贷款建设的太阳能热水器。

Police family district in the suburb of Harare, Zimbabwe installs solar water heaters purchased with interest−free loans from China.

2. 2015 年 9 月，习近平主席在联合国可持续发展峰会上宣布，中国将设立南南合作援助基金。图为联合国总部大楼外可持续发展目标宣传画面。

President Xi Jinping announced the establishment of South− South Cooperation Fund at the UN Sustainable Development Summit in Sep. 2015. The photo shows the UN headquarter advocating for sustainable development.

1. 联合国世界粮食计划署用中国政府南南合作援助基金采购的小麦等物资运抵索马里。
Wheat and other in-kind assistance purchased by the World Food Program with cash assistance from China being shipped to Somalia.

2. 2016年4月，南南合作与发展学院的成立，标志着中国与南南国家的合作从资金和工程支持转向发展智慧和发展理念的交流。图为2017年7月南南合作与发展学院首届硕士生毕业合影。
In Apr. 2016, the Institute of South-South Cooperation and Development was established, marking that the cooperation between China and other countries of the Global South has evolved from funding and engineering support to exchanges of development wisdom and philosophy. The photo shows the commencement ceremony of the first class of graduates of the Institute in Jul. 2017.

支持基础设施建设
Support Infrastructure Development

中国帮助发展中国家建设了大量基础设施，包括道路、桥梁、铁路、机场、港口、电站和通信网络等经济基础设施。

China supports other developing countries in infrastructure development in road, bridge, railway, airport, port, power station and telecommunications network.

1
2

1. 中国援建的尼日尔津德尔供水项目落成后，城市百余万人喝上了自来水。图为蓝宝石状水塔下，尼日尔百姓欢呼雀跃。

Millions of people in Niger get access to running water after the China-assisted water supply project was completed in Zinder. The photo shows the exaltation of Nigeriens under the gem-shaped water tower.

2. 2018 年 8 月，由中国援建的中马友谊大桥正式通车。这座跨海大桥全长约两公里，将对马尔代夫经济、社会的发展发挥重要作用。

In Aug. 2018, the China-assisted China-Maldives Friendship Bridge was open to traffic, contributing to the economic and social development of the Maldives. The photo shows the China-Maldives Friendship Bridge.

1
2

1. 2010 年 11 月，中国援建的莫桑比克马普托国际机场新航站楼正式启用。
In Nov. 2010, the China-assisted terminal building of the Maputo International Airport in Mozambique went into operation.

2. 中国援建的非洲联盟会议中心被誉为中非传统友谊和新时期合作的里程碑。图为位于埃塞俄比亚首都亚的斯亚贝巴的非盟会议中心。
The China-assisted AU Conference Center is reputed as a milestone for the China-Africa traditional friendship and cooperation in the new era. The photo shows the AU Conference Center in Addis Ababa, Ethiopia.

助力农业发展

Promote Agricultural Development

中国帮助发展中国家建设农场、兴修水利，并派专家提供农业技术服务。

China has helped other developing countries build farms and hydropower projects, and sent experts to provide agricultural technology service.

	1
2	3

1. 2001 年 12 月，中国援助的莫桑比克贝拉海水养虾项目竣工试生产。图为养虾池及收获的养殖对虾。

In Dec. 2001, the China-assisted shrimp mariculture program was completed and went into trial production in Beira, Mozambique. The photo shows the shrimp pond and the farmed prawns.

2. 2015 年 5 月，中国援建老挝沙湾拿吉省色萨拉龙—赛格灌溉项目引水干渠。

In May. 2015, the China-assisted Xesalalong-Saige irrigation project in Savannakhét Laos was completed.

3. 吉尔吉斯斯坦当地人翘指称赞中国援助的农机。

A Kyrgyz gives a thumbs-up to China-assisted agricultural machinery.

1
2

1. 2016 年 4 月，中国援科特迪瓦农业水稻技术组向当地稻农讲解水稻种植技术。
China's rice technology group explaining rice cultivation techniques to local farmers in Cote d'Ivoire, Apr. 2016.

2. 袁隆平院士和国外专家在田间交流杂交水稻种植技术。
Yuan Longping, famous Chinese agronomist discussing rice cultivation technologies with foreign experts in the field.

改善医疗卫生条件
Improve Healthcare Conditions
中国为发展中国家建设医疗设施、提供医疗设备和药品，并派遣医疗队提供医疗服务。
China has built medical facilities, provided medical equipment and medicines, and sent medical teams to other developing countries.

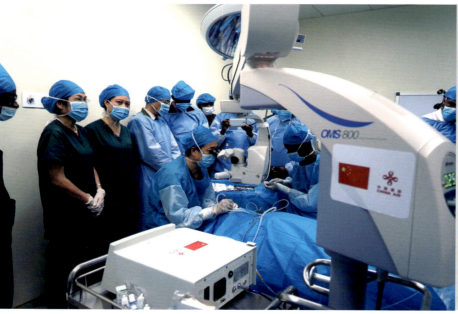

1	2
3	

1. 2017 年 8 月，中国政府援建的埃塞俄比亚蒂鲁内什—北京医院。
The China-assisted Tirunesh-Beijing Hospital, Aug. 2017.

2. 2014 年 11 月，中国援建的利比里亚埃博拉出血热诊疗中心。
The China-assisted Ebola Hemorrhagic Fever Treatment Center in Liberia, Nov. 2014.

3. "光明行" 医疗队已实施近万例白内障复明手术。图为 2016 年 5 月，中国医疗队赴岛国科摩罗开展 "光明行" 活动。
The Brightness Action medical team has performed near 10,000 operations for cataract patients. The photo shows the Chinese Brightness Action medical team in Comoros, May 2016.

聚焦
辉煌
Focus on Brilliant Achievements
40周年

1 | 2
3

1. 2016 年 4 月，中国援非医疗队员在突尼斯西迪·布济德省下乡义诊。
China's Charity Clinic in rural area of Sidi Bouzid, Tunisia, Apr. 2016.

2. 中国首支援助巴基斯坦医疗队队员在瓜达尔检查救护车设备。
A member of the first Chinese medical team to Gwadar, Pakistan checking ambulance equipment.

3. 2014 年，中国向埃博拉疫情严重的部分西非国家提供医用防护服、消毒药剂、测温仪、药品等抗击疫情所急需的物资。
In 2014, China provided in-kind assistance of medical protective clothing, disinfectant, thermo detector, and medicine to West African countries stricken by Ebola.

促进生态环境保护
Promote Environmental Protection

中国帮助发展中国家开发小水电，并传授沼气、
太阳能等清洁能源开发利用技术。

China has helped other developing countries build
small hydropower plants and shared clean energy
technologies in biogas and solar power.

1	2
	3

1. 2013年11月，中国企业捐建的古巴1兆瓦并网光伏电站项目正式
并网发电。图为工作人员在检查太阳能电池板。
In Nov. 2013, the 1 MW PV power program, donated by Chinese
companies to Cuba, was formally connected to the grid. The photo
shows workers checking the solar panels.

2. 2009年底，中国沼气系统在汤加成功开通。
At the end of 2009, the China-assisted biogas system went into
operation in Tonga.

3. 2016年9月，中国在肯尼亚援建的中非联合研究中心正式移交，成
为中国与肯尼亚乃至与整个非洲大陆在生物多样性保护、生态环境监测
等领域开展科技合作和人才培养的重要平台。
The China-African Joint Research Center in Kenya, assisted by China
in Sep. 2016, has become an important platform for technology
cooperation in biodiversity and ecological monitoring and talent
cultivation between China and Kenya and even the African continent.

促进文化教育发展

Promote Cultural Development and Education

中国重视对发展中国家文化教育领域的援助，包括建设文化设施及学校，提供文教用品和设备，派遣教师、艺术家，资助留学生来华学习等。

China is committed to assisting other developing countries in culture and education, in the form of building cultural facilities and schools, providing stationery and education equipment, sending teachers and artists, and granting scholarship to study in China.

```
        1
        ──┬──
          │
          2
```

1. 2018 年 10 月，学生在中国企业援建的塔吉克斯坦杜尚别学校内上课。
Students in the China–assisted school in Dushanbe, Tajikistan, Oct. 2018.

2. 2006 年 11 月，中国与黎巴嫩圣约瑟夫大学签订合作建立孔子学院的正式协议。图为孔子学院少儿班课堂观摩。
In Nov. 2006, China and Saint Joseph University of Lebanon officially signed the agreement to open a Confucius Institute. The photo shows a teenagers' class of the Institute.

1	2
3	

1. 2011 年 9 月，中国青年志愿者向欧洲青年介绍中国书法。
A Chinese volunteer introducing Chinese calligraphy to European youth, Sep. 2011.

2. 2004 年 7 月，埃塞俄比亚留学生在天津工程师范学院学习班开班仪式上。
Students from Ethiopia at the commencement of the Tianjin University of Technology and Education, Jul. 2004.

3. 2007 年 12 月，游人在古巴首都哈瓦那由中国援建的游乐园内游玩。
Tourists enjoying themselves at the China-assisted amusement park in Havana, Cuba, Dec. 2007.

提供人道主义援助
Provide Humanitarian Assistance

中国长期积极帮助相关国家有效应对各种灾害和冲突，及时提供人道主义援助，支持灾后重建。

China has long helped countries in need with disaster relief and conflict resolution and provided humanitarian assistance in support of post-conflict reconstruction.

2010年2月，中国赴海地维和警察防暴队队员帮助当地居民领取救济粮食。
A Chinese peacekeeper of the riot control team in Haiti helping a local resident carry relief food, Feb. 2010.

聚焦 辉煌
Focus on Brilliant Achievements

40周年

1. 2010 年 11 月，中国派灾后重建考察小组访问巴基斯坦。图为中国商务部官员等在巴基斯坦听取当地公路局人员介绍灾情。
In Nov. 2010, China sent a post-disaster reconstruction group to Pakistan. The photo shows officials from the Ministry of Commerce listening to the briefing about the disaster by staff of the road bureau.

2. 2016 年 5 月，厄瓜多尔少年在中国政府援助的临时帐篷前玩耍。
A boy in Ecuador playing in front of the relief tent donated by China, May. 2016.

帮助提升自主发展能力

Capacity Building for Self-driven Development

中国采取多种形式帮助发展中国家加强能力建设，包括提供单项技术援助、开展技术合作、举办技术培训班和官员研修班等。

China has helped other developing countries with capacity building in various ways, including individual technology assistance, technology cooperation, technology workshops, and seminars for officials.

1. 2014 年 8 月，来自津巴布韦的学员在北京举行的发展中国家农产品流通体系建设研修班上听取授课。
Students from Zimbabwe attending a class on the agricultural produce circulation system in developing countries, Beijing, Aug. 2014.

2. 2014 年 3 月，黑山援助项目管理人员研修班学员和老师等在结业典礼上合影。
Group photo of students and teachers of the training course on assistance program management for the Republic of Montenegro, Mar. 2014.

1. 2013 年 9 月，由商务部主办、宁夏农林科学院承办的"阿拉伯国家防沙治沙技术培训班"在宁夏回族自治区银川市开班。图为学员在宁夏盐池县毛乌素沙地边缘参观。

In Sep. 2013, the training course on desertification prevention and control for Arab countries, organized by the Ministry of Commerce and enforced by Ningxia Academy of Agriculture and Forestry Sciences was launched in Yinchuan, Ningxia Hui Autonomous Region. The photo shows students visiting the Mu Us Sandy Land in the county of Yanchi, Ningxia.

2. 2018 年 8 月，纳米比亚的农业科技官员在甘肃省民勤县治沙综合试验站学习制作草方格沙障。

Agro-technology officials from Namibia learning to make straw checkerboard sand barriers at the desertification control station of Minqin County, Gansu province, Aug. 2018.

加入世贸组织后，中国切实履行承诺，积极参与多哈回合谈判，成为多边贸易体制的建设者、维护者和贡献者，国际贸易规则的重要参与者，为全球经济治理贡献中国智慧。

Since the accession to the WTO, China has been devoted to comply with its obligations and to actively participate in Doha negotiations. China has been a supporter, guard, and contributor to the multilateral trading system. China shares its wisdom with global economic governance and has become an important player in the making of international trading rules.

第六章　全面融入世界经贸体系

Chapter 6　Integration into the World Economic and Trading System

从复关到加入

The Resumption of China's GATT Contracting Party Status to China's WTO Accession

中国是世界贸易组织（World Trade Organization, WTO）的前身——关税与贸易总协定 (General Agreement on Tariffs and Trade, GATT) 的创始缔约方。从 1986 年提出"复关"起，中国经历 15 年艰辛谈判，终于在 2001 年加入世贸组织。

China was a founding Contracting Party to the General Agreement on Tariffs and Trade (GATT), the predecessor of World Trade Organization (WTO). China applied for resumption of its GATT Contracting Party Status in 1986. After 15 years of difficult negotiations, China joined the WTO in 2001.

1986 年 7 月，中国照会关贸总协定总干事邓克尔，申请恢复中国关贸总协定缔约国地位。图为中国恢复关贸总协定缔约国地位的申请书。

In Jul. 1986, China notified to GATT Director-General Dunkel to apply for the resumption of China's GATT Contracting Party status. The picture shows the application note of China.

世界贸易组织总干事
鲁杰罗先生：

忆及中国为1947年关贸总协定创始缔约方之一和1986年7月10日的中国恢复在关贸总协定中的缔约方地位的申请，考虑到中国全面参加了乌拉圭回合多边贸易谈判并签署了《最后文件》和《建立世界贸易组织协议》，我奉政府之命通知总干事阁下：中国政府决定根据《世界贸易组织协议》第十二条申请加入世界贸易组织，并要求将现有"关贸总协定中国缔约方问题工作组"更名为"中国加入世界贸易组织工作组"。

顺致敬意！

中华人民共和国
常驻代表、大使

一九九五年十一月二十八日

MISSION PERMANENTE DE LA RÉPUBLIQUE POPULAIRE DE CHINE
A GENÈVE
11, CHEMIN DE SURVILLE · 1213 PETIT-LANCY, GENÈVE
TÉL. (022) 92 25 48 · 92 25 48

WTO/95/08   (Translation)

Geneva, 28 November 1995

Your Excellency,

Recalling that China is one of the original contracting parties of the GATT 1947 and that China applied for the resumption of its contracting party status to GATT on 10 July 1986;

Recalling further that China is a full participant in the Uruguay Round multilateral trade negotiations and a signatory to the Final Act and the WTO Agreement;

Upon instructions of my government, I have the honour to inform you that the Government of the People's Republic of China has decided to request accession to the World Trade Organization (WTO) under Article XII of the WTO Agreement and the consequent transformation of the existing GATT Working Party on China's Status as a Contracting Party into a WTO Accession Working Party.

Please accept, Your Excellency, the assurances of my highest consideration.

JIN Yongjian (signed)
Ambassador
Permanent Representative
of the People's Republic of China

H.E. Mr. Renato Ruggiero
Director-General
World Trade Organization
GENEVA

1
2

1. 1995年11月，中国政府代表向世贸组织总干事鲁杰罗递交中国加入世贸组织申请书，中国复关谈判转为加入谈判。图为中国加入世贸组织申请书。
In Nov.1995, representatives of the Chinese Government submitted the application for China's accession to the WTO Director-General Rugero. China's resumption negotiations turned into accession negotiations. The picture shows the application for China's accession to the WTO.

2. 1995年1月，世贸组织成立，取代了运行近半个世纪的关税与贸易总协定。图为世贸组织办公大楼。
The WTO was founded in Jan. 1995, replacing the General Agreement on Tariffs and Trade which had been in operation for half a century. The picture shows the office building of the WTO.

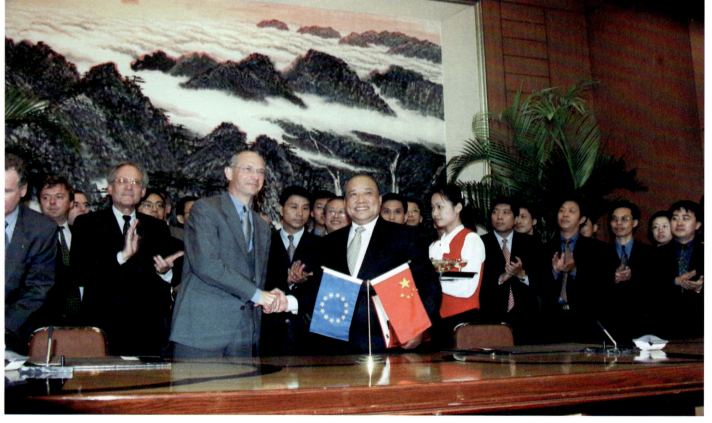

1. 1999 年 11 月，中美双方在北京进行了六天六夜的谈判，终于在 11 月 15 日达成了双边市场准入协议。图为中美双方签署协议现场。

In Nov. 1999, China and the United States held negotiations in Beijing for six days and nights. Finally a bilateral agreement on market access was reached on Nov. 15. The picture shows the signing of the agreement by China and the United States.

2. 自 2000 年初起，中欧之间进行了多轮磋商。双方最终于 2000 年 5 月 19 日达成双边市场准入协议。图为中欧双方签署协议现场。

Since the beginning of 2000, several rounds of consultations between China and Europe took place. A bilateral market access agreement was finally reached on May 19, 2000. The picture shows the signing of the agreement by China and Europe.

1 | 2
3

1. 2001 年 11 月，世贸组织第四届部长级会议主席贾迈勒一"槌"定音，宣布通过中国加入世界贸易组织的决议。
Youssef Hussain Kamal of Qatar, Chairman of the 4th WTO Ministerial Conference, announced the accession of China to the WTO on Nov. 2001.

2. 举杯庆贺中国加入世界贸易组织。
Participants ra sed their glasses to congratulate China's accession to the WTO.

3. 世界贸易组织第四届部长级会议所在地——多哈喜来登酒店。
Sheraton Hotel where the 4th WTO Ministerial Conference was held in Doha.

参与世贸组织多哈回合谈判
Active Participation in WTO Doha Negotiations

中国积极参与多哈回合谈判，在多哈回合最重要的农业、非农产品市场准入、服务业等议题上提出中方参与谈判的立场和主张，为多哈回合谈判取得成果作出了积极贡献。

China actively participates in Doha Round negotiations, by presenting China's position and views on vital issues such as agricultural and non−agricultural market access, services and others. China has been contributing to the Doha negotiations in a constructive way.

1
—
2

1. 2005 年 12 月，中国香港主办了世贸组织第六届部长级会议。
In Dec. 2005, Hong Kong SAR China hosted the 6th Ministerial conference of the WTO.

2. 2009 年 12 月，时任商务部部长陈德铭在世贸组织第七届部长级会议上指出，中国始终是多边贸易体制的坚定支持者，始终是自由贸易原则的忠实维护者，始终是多哈谈判的积极推动者。
In Dec. 2009, Chen Deming, the then Minister of Commerce, stated at the 7th Ministerial Conference of the WTO that China is always a firm supporter of the multilateral trading system, a faithful defender of free trade principles and an active promoter of the Doha Round.

1
2

1. 2013 年 12 月，世贸组织第九届部长级会议在印尼巴厘岛举行，中国为推动达成多哈回合"早期收获"一揽子协议作出了突出贡献。
In Dec. 2013, the 9th Ministerial Conference of the WTO was held in Bali, Indonesia. China made important contribution to the Doha early harvest. Agreements were made in areas of trade facilitation, agriculture and development.

2. 2017 年 12 月，世贸组织第十一届部长级会议上，中国专门召集了欧盟、日本、加拿大、巴西等 70 多个世贸成员参加的投资便利化早餐会。图为中国商务部部长钟山在世贸组织第十一届部长级会议上发言。
In Dec. 2017, at the 11th Ministerial Conference of the WTO, China convened a breakfast meeting, promoting investment facilitation. More than 70 WTO members attended, including the EU, Japan, Canada and Brazil. The picture shows Zhong Shan, the Minister of Commerce, speaking at the 11th WTO Ministerial Conference.

支持多边贸易体制

Support the Multilateral Trading System

加入世贸组织后，中国积极参与世贸组织各项工作，认真履行成员义务，努力确保国内相关立法和政策与世贸组织规则相一致，做多边贸易体制的坚定维护者。

Upon the accession to the WTO, China actively participates in all WTO work, fulfills its obligations as a member, strives to align relevant domestic legislation and policies with WTO rules, and firmly defends the multilateral trading system.

1 |
---|---
2 |

1. 2017 年 8 月，金砖国家第七次经贸部长会议在上海开幕。商务部部长钟山表示，会议聚焦投资便利化、促进贸易发展、加强经济技术合作和能力建设、支持多边贸易体制等议题。

In Aug. 2017, the 7th Meeting of the BRICS Trade Ministers was held in Shanghai. ZhongShan, Minister of Commerce stated that the meeting focused on investment facilitation, trade growth, enhanced economic technical cooperation and capacity building, and supporting the multilateral trading system.

2. 2018 年 6 月，为全面介绍中国履行加入世贸组织承诺的实践，阐释中国参与多边贸易体制建设的原则立场和政策主张，中国政府特发表《中国与世界贸易组织》白皮书。图为《中国与世界贸易组织》白皮书。

In Jun. 2018, in order to elaborate on China's practices of fulfilling its WTO commitments, and to explain China's position and policies on building the multilateral trade system, the Chinese government published a White Paper on *China and the World Trade Organization*.The picture shows the published White Paper.

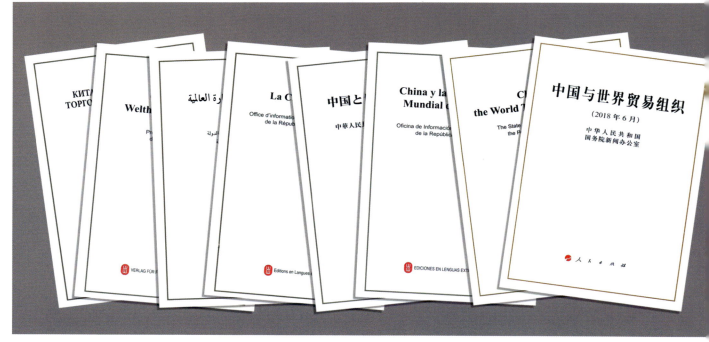

```
1 |
2 |
3 |
```

1. 中国与 60 多个成员联署提案，推动启动世贸组织上诉机构大法官遴选程序。左图为首位中国籍上诉机构大法官张月姣，右图为中国籍上诉机构现任大法官赵宏。

Together with more than 60 WTO members, China submitted a proposal on resuming the selection process of Appellate Body members. The picture on the left shows Ms. Zhang Yuejiao, who is the first member of the WTO Appellate Body from China. The right picture shows Ms. Zhao Hong, who is the current member of the WTO Appellate Body from China.

2. 中国通过世贸组织机制已向其他成员提出多项经贸关注，如欧盟滥用贸易救济措施等。2011 年 4 月起，欧盟正式取消对中国皮鞋征收的高额反倾销税。图为比利时布鲁塞尔一家服装店前摆放着中国特色的鞋子。

China raised a number of economic and trade concerns to other members in the WTO, such as the abuse of trade remedy measures by the EU. On Apr. 2011, the EU stopped implementing anti-dumping duties on the imports of Chinese leather shoes. The picture shows shoes with distinct Chinese style in a boutique in Brussels, Belgium.

3. 2011 年 7 月，世贸组织上诉机构发布中国起诉欧盟对华碳钢紧固件反倾销措施案的裁决报告，认定欧盟《反倾销基本条例》第 9(5) 条规定违反世贸规则。图为中国抗辩小组成员赴欧洲拜访欧盟对外贸易协会。

In Jul. 2011, the WTO Appellate Body released the report on the case brought by China against the EU on anti-Dumping Measures on Certain Iron or Steel Fasteners. It finds that Article 9 (5) of the EU *Basic Anti-Dumping Regulation* was not consistent with the WTO rules. The picture shows the members of the Chinese defense team visiting the Foreign Trade Association of the EU.

参与全球经济治理体系改革和建设
Active Participation in Reforming and Developing Global Economic Governance System

中国明确提出"共商共建共享"的全球治理新理念，以"一带一路"由中国倡议成为世界共识、G20 杭州峰会和金砖国家领导人厦门会晤等为标志，确立了中国积极参与全球经济治理的新方向。

China has proposed the new global governance ideal of extensive consultation, joint contribution and shared benefits. The Belt and Road evolving from a Chinese initiative to world consensus, the G20 Hangzhou Summit and the BRICS Xiamen Summit are all symbols for China's active participation in global economic governance.

1

2

1. 中国作为 2014 年亚太经合组织领导人非正式会议的东道主，努力推进和引领亚太自贸区进程。图为北京怀柔雁栖湖湖心岛 APEC 峰会日出东方大酒店。
As the host of the 2014 APEC Economic Leaders' Meeting, China strives to advance and lead the process of the Free Trade Area of the Asia-Pacific. The picture shows the Sunrise East Kempinski Hotel for the APEC Summit near the Yanqi Lake in the Huairou District of Beijing.

2. 2016 年 9 月，习近平主席在二十国集团工商峰会开幕式上，首次全面阐释中国的全球经济治理观。
In Sep. 2016, at the opening ceremony of the B20 Summit, President Xi Jinping comprehensively explained China's view on global economic governance for the first time.

1. 2018 年 6 月，上合组织青岛峰会在青岛召开。习近平主席提出发展、安全、合作、文明和全球治理"五观"。图为青岛市南区的一处花坛。
In Jun. 2018, the SCO Qingdao Summit was held in Qingdao. President Xi Jinping proposed the outlooks on development, security, cooperation, civilization and global governance. The picture shows a flowerbed in the Southern District of Qingdao.

2. 2017 年 9 月，金砖国家领导人峰会在中国厦门举行。习近平主席在厦门峰会上正式提出"金砖 +"合作模式。图为金砖国家领导人峰会（厦门）场地外景。
In Sep. 2017, the BRICS summit was held in Xiamen, China. During the Summit, President Xi Jinping proposed the "BRICS+" cooperation mechanism. The picture shows the outdoor scene of the Xiamen BRICS summit.

参与区域和次区域经济合作
Active Participation in Regional and Sub-regional Economic Cooperation

中国与周边国家和地区签署自贸协定或签订双边投资协定，并积极开展次区域经济合作。

China has signed FTAs or bilateral investment agreements with neighboring countries and regions and has actively conducted sub-regional economic cooperation.

❶ 多边合作
Multilateral Cooperation

中非合作。2000年，中非双方共同创立了中非合作论坛。截至目前，论坛已累计举办了7届部长级会议，其中2006、2015和2018年升格为峰会。

China-Africa cooperation. In 2000, China and Africa jointly launched the Forum on China-Africa cooperation. Up to now, the forum has held 7 ministerial meetings, of which 2006, 2015 and 2018 were upgraded to summits.

1

—

2

1. 2006年，中非合作论坛标牌及花坛。
The sign and flowerbed for the 2006 Forum on China-Africa Cooperation.

2. 2018年中非合作论坛北京峰会场景。
The 2018 Beijing Summit for the Forum on China-Africa Cooperation.

1
—
2

1. 东盟"10+1"合作。2017年9月，东亚合作经贸部长系列会议在菲律宾首都马尼拉举行，中国商务部部长钟山率团出席会议。
ASEAN "10+1" cooperation. In Sep. 2017, the Economic and Trade Ministers' meetings for East Asian Cooperation were held in Manila, the capital of the Philippines. The Minister of Commerce, Zhong Shan, led a delegation to the meeting.

2. "16+1"合作。左图为2018年6月，第三次中国—中东欧国家经贸促进部长级会议在宁波举行。右图为首个"16+1"经贸合作示范区在宁波正式启动建设。
"16+1" cooperation. The left picture shows that the 3rd Ministerial Conference of China and Central and Eastern European Countries on Promoting Trade and Economic Cooperation was held in Ningbo in Jun. 2018. The right picture shows the launch of the first "16+1" demonstration area for business cooperation in Ningbo.

❷ 区域经济一体化
Regional Economic Integration

目前中国已与 25 个国家和地区达成 17 个自贸协定。
China has concluded 17 FTA negotiations with 25 countries or regions.

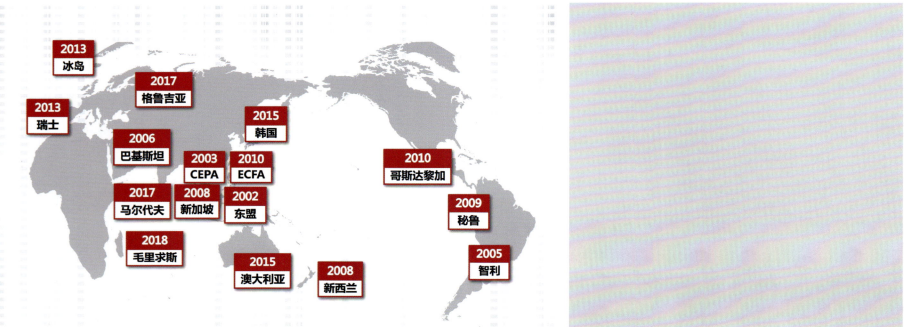

2013 冰岛

2013 瑞士

2017 格鲁吉亚

2015 韩国

2006 巴基斯坦

2003 CEPA

2010 ECFA

2010 哥斯达黎加

2017 马尔代夫

2008 新加坡

2002 东盟

2009 秘鲁

2018 毛里求斯

2015 澳大利亚

2008 新西兰

2005 智利

```
1
——
 2
```

1. 中国自由贸易区建设起步于2002年，迄今已与 22 个国家达成了 14 个自由贸易协定。此外，内地与港澳签署了 CEPA，海峡两岸签署了 ECFA。
China started its FTA practice in 2002, and has entered into 14 FTAs with 22 countries. China's mainland signed CEPA with Hong Kong and Macao. The two sides of the Taiwan Straits signed ECFA.

2. 2010 年 1 月，中国建立最早、覆盖人口最多、涉及贸易额最大的自贸区中国—东盟自贸区正式建成。图为中国—东盟自由贸易区建成庆祝仪式在广西南宁举行。
In Jan. 2010, China–ASEAN FTA was established, which is the first FTA of China covering the largest population and the largest trade volume. The photo shows the ceremony in Nanning, Guangxi Province to celebrate the establishment of the FTA.

热烈庆祝中国－东盟自由贸易区建成
Celebration on the Establishment of China-ASEAN Free Trade Area

1. 中国已与 13 个 "一带一路" 共建国家签署自由贸易协定。图为 2017 年 5 月，"一带一路" 国际合作高峰论坛期间，中国与格鲁吉亚举行自由贸易协定谈判。

China has signed FTAs with 13 countries along Belt and Road. The picture shows that during the Belt and Road Forum for International Cooperation in May. 2017, China and Georgia were having FTA negotiations.

2. 中欧投资协定谈判于 2014 年 1 月启动，截至 2018 年 7 月已进行 18 轮谈判。图为在北京举行的第 30 届中欧经贸混委会。

The negotiations on investment agreement between China and Europe started in Jan. 2014. Eighteen rounds of negotiations have been held by Jul. 2018. The picture shows the 30th China-EU Joint Economic and Trade Commission in Beijing.

1
2

2014 年 7 月，中国—瑞士自贸协定生效。图为首批来自中国的零关税货物抵达瑞士巴塞尔。
In Jul. 2014, China–Switzerland FTA entered into force. The photo shows that the first batch of Chinese products which were duty–free according to the agreement arrived in Basel, Switzerland.

1　2

3

1. 2017 年 6 月，商务部与香港特区政府在《内地与香港关于建立更紧密经贸关系的安排》（CEPA）下的《投资协议》和《经济技术合作协议》签约仪式在香港举行。

In Jun. 2017, the Signing Ceremony of *Investment Agreement* and *Agreement on Economic and Technical Cooperation* under CEPA between MOFCOM and Hong Kong SAR government was held in Hong Kong.

2. 2017 年 12 月，商务部与澳门特区政府在《内地与澳门关于建立更紧密经贸关系的安排》（CEPA）下的《投资协议》和《经济技术合作协议》签约仪式在澳门举行。

In Dec. 2017, the Signing Ceremony of *Investment Agreement* and *Agreement on Economic and Technical Cooperation* under CEPA between MOFCOM and Macao SAR government was held in Macao.

3. 2010 年 7 月，台湾两岸和平发展论坛在台北举办大型群众集会，支持和庆祝《海峡两岸经济合作框架协议》（ECFA）完成签署，上千名来自台湾各界的群众挤满了位于福华文教会馆的会场。

In Jul. 2010, the Cross-Strait Peaceful Development Forum held a large mass rally in Taipei in support and celebration of the signing of *ECFA*. About 1,000 people from all walks of life filled the venue in Howard Civil Service International House.

❸ 次区域合作
Sub-regional Economic Cooperation

中国主要参与图们江、大湄公河、中亚次区域经济合作。
China mainly participates in Great Tumen, Great Mekong and Central Asia sub-regional economic cooperation.

2014 年 9 月，大图们倡议第十五次政府间协商委员会部长级会议在吉林省延边朝鲜族自治州召开。
In Sept. 2014, the 15th Consultative Commission Meeting of the Greater Tumen Initiative was held in Yanbian Korean Autonomous Prefecture, Jilin Province.

1 / 2

1. 2014 年 11 月，中亚区域经济合作第 13 次部长级会议在吉尔吉斯斯坦首都都比什凯克举行。
In Nov. 2014, the 13th ministerial meeting of the Central Asia Regional Economic Cooperation was held in Bishkek, the capital of Kyrgyzstan.

2. 2015 年 6 月，第七届大湄公河次区域经济走廊论坛在云南昆明举行。时任中国商务部部长高虎城出席论坛开幕式并致辞。
In Jun. 2015, the 7th Economic Corridors Forum of the Greater Mekong Subregion (GMS) Economic Cooperation Program was held in Kunming, Yunnan. Gao Hucheng, the Minister of Commerce then, addressed the opening ceremony of the Forum.

第三篇 历程回顾

回首四十年风云激荡，我们遇到过困难，遭到过挑战，但我们不懈奋斗、与时俱进，用勤劳、勇敢、智慧书写了当代中国对外经贸发展的新篇章。

Part III　Review of the Past

During the past four decades of ups and downs, we have worked tirelessly and kept up with the times despite all the difficulties and challenges we met. We have written a new chapter of contemporary China's foreign trade and economic development with our diligence, courage and wisdom.

以试点为特征的开放突破期，实现了对长期封闭体制与计划经济的"突围"，通过创办经济特区、经济技术开发区，开放 14 个沿海城市、沿海经济开放区等尝试，为经济体制改革提供了样板和经验。

During this period featuring pilot programs, China managed to "break out" of its long-standing closed system and planning economy. Pilot programs such as setting up special economic zones and economic and technological development zones as well as opening up 14 coastal cities and coastal economic areas provided China's economic reform with feasible models and experience.

第一章 国门初开（1978—1992）
Chapter 1　Early Opening up (1978–1992)

召开十一届三中全会
The Third Plenary Session of the 11th CPC Central Committee

1978 年 12 月，党的十一届三中全会作出实行改革开放的重大决策。左图为十一届三中全会会场，右图为山东青岛市兰山路礼堂正在召开传达学习十一届三中全会精神的大会。

The 11th CPC Central Committee decided to embark on reform and opening-up at its third plenary session in Dec. 1978. The picture on the left shows the venue of the session and the picture on the right shows a meeting on learning the spirit of the third plenary session of the 11th CPC Central Committee was held at the assembly hall on Lanshan Street, Qingdao, Shandong province.

设立四个经济特区
Setting up Four Special Economic Zones (SEZs)

1979年7月，中共中央决定在深圳、珠海、汕头和厦门试办特区。

In Jul. 1979, the CPC Central Committee decided to set up pilot SEZs in Shenzhen, Zhuhai, Shantou and Xiamen.

1
—
2

1. 1979年"开山炮"在深圳蛇口炸响。
In 1979, the ground-breaking blast in Shekou, Shenzhen heralded China's reform and opening-up.

2. 1982年深圳蛇口工业区。
Shekou (Shenzhen) industrial zone in 1982.

1

2

1. 与香港一河之隔的深圳渔民村。
A fishing village in Shenzhen connected with Hong Kong by a river.

2. 2018 年的深圳渔民村。
A fishing village in Shenzhen(2018).

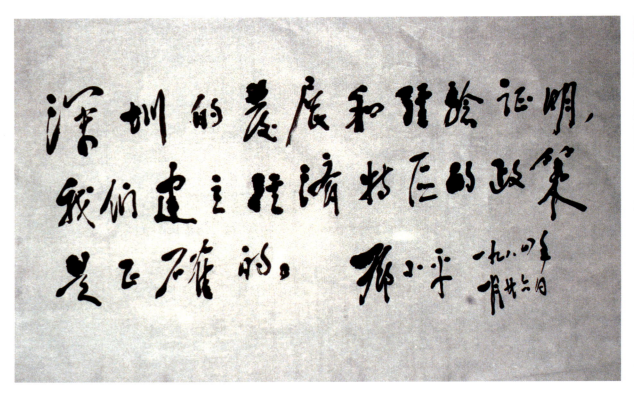

1. 1984 年 1 月，邓小平同志视察深圳经济特区时为特区题字。
Deng Xiaoping's inscription during his inspection of the Shenzhen special zone in Jan. 1984.
2. 深圳特区打工妹。
Female migrant workers in Shenzhen special zone.
3. 1980 年 5 月，"特区"被正式定名为"经济特区"。图为深圳蛇口工业区女工。
In May. 1980, the special zone was renamed "special economic zone". The picture shows the female workers in Shekou industrial zone in Shenzhen.

1	
2	3

1
2

1. 1985 年珠海特区一角。
Zhuhai special zone (1985).

2. 2017 年珠海拱北口岸夜景。
 Night view of Gongbei port, Zhuhai (2017).

1. 1982 年汕头港一角。
Shantou port (1982).

2. 2017 年汕头市新风貌。
Shantou's new look (2017).

1. 1991 年位于厦门东渡的新港区。
New port area in Dongdu, Xiamen (1991).

2. 2016 年厦门海沧新貌。
The new appearance of Haicang，Xiamen（2016）.

开发开放上海浦东新区
Developing and Opening up Pudong District, Shanghai

1990 年 4 月, 中共中央决定开发和开放上海浦东新区。
In Apr. 1990, the CPC Central Committee and the State Council officially
announced the decision to develop and open up Pudong District, Shanghai.

1
2

1. 1995 年上海浦东陆家嘴金融贸易区。
Lujiazui financial and trace zone, Pudong District, Shanghai (1995).

2. 2005 年上海洋山深水港无人码头。
Unmanned wharf at Yangshan deep-water port, Shanghai (2005).

2017 年上海黄浦江两岸夜景。
Night view along the Huangpu River, Shanghai (2017).

开放 14 个沿海港口城市

Opening up 14 Coastal Port Cities

1984 年 3 月，中共中央书记处和国务院联合召开沿海部分城市座谈会，建议进一步开放大连、秦皇岛、天津、烟台、青岛、连云港、南通、上海、宁波、温州、福州、广州、湛江、北海共 14 个沿海港口城市。

In Mar. 1984, the Secretariat of the CPC Central Committee and the State Council held a seminar to discuss the development of some coastal cities, proposing to further open up 14 coastal port cities, namely, Dalian, Qinhuangdao, Tianjin, Yantai, Qingdao, Lianyungang, Nantong, Shanghai, Ningbo, Wenzhou, Fuzhou, Guangzhou, Zhanjiang and Beihai.

	2	3
1		

1. 20 世纪 80 年代，中国自行建造的第一艘 5 万吨级远洋货轮 "西湖" 号在大连红旗造船厂建成下水。

In the 1980s, Xihu (West Lake) vessel, the first 50,000–tonne oceangoing freighter made independently by China was launched in Dalian.

2. 2018 年秦皇岛市金梦海湾广场。

Golden Dream Bay Plaza, Qinhuangdao, 2018.

3. 2007 年秦皇岛市区街景。

City view of Qinhuangdao, 2007.

1 │
2

1. 1985 年连云港码头。
Wharf at Lianyungang port, 1985.

2. 中—哈（连云港）物流基地和集装箱码头。
China–Kazakhstan (Lianyungang) logistics base
and container terminal.

1. 1978 年宁波北仑港区开发建设启动时的爆破画面。
Demolition at the launching event of the development of Beilun port area, Ningbo (1978).

2. 2018 年宁波舟山港穿山港区集装箱码头。
Container wharf, Chuanshan port area, Zhoushan port, Ningbo (2018).

开辟三个沿海经济开发区
Opening up Three Coastal Economic Zones

1985 年 2 月，开放长三角、珠三角、闽南厦漳泉三角地区，是我国实施对内搞活经济、对外实行开放的又一重要步骤。

In Feb. 1985, opening up the Yangtze River Delta, the Pearl River Delta and the Golden Triangle of Xiamen, Zhangzhou and Quanzhou in southern Fujian province, is another important step in the implementation of invigorating the domestic economy and opening to the outside world policy.

2008 年 5 月，杭州湾跨海大桥正式建成通车，对浙江省乃至长三角南翼地区的整体发展产生积极影响。

The opening of the Hangzhou Bay ocean-crossing bridge in May. 2008 contributed to the overall development of Zhejiang province and the southern wing of the Yangtze River Delta.

舟山背靠长三角广阔经济腹地，是我国东部沿海和长江流域走向世界的主要海上门户。图为 2013 年舟山东港新区全景。
With the Yangtze River Delta as its broad economic hinterland, Zhoushan is a major gateway connecting China's coastal region in the east and the Yangtze River Basin to the world. Above s a panorama of East Port New Area, Zhoushan in 2013.

2018 年 10 月，港珠澳大桥通车，推动粤港澳大湾区建设成为更具活力的经济区。
The Hong Kong–Zhuhai–Macao Bridge was opened in Oct. 2018 to build the Guangdong–Hong Kong–Macao Greater Bay Area into a more dynamic economic area.

2015 年 5 月，泉州湾大桥建成通车。
Quanzhou Bay Bridge was opened in May. 2015.

开放辽东半岛、胶东半岛
Opening up the Liaodong Peninsula and Jiaodong Peninsula

1988 年初，中国开放辽东半岛、胶东半岛。

China opened up the Liaodong Peninsula and Jiaodong Peninsula at the beginning of 1988.

1

2

1. 早期辽宁丹东至山东烟台新增客运航班。
Newly–opened passenger ferries from Dandong, Liaoning province to Yantai, Shandong province in the past.

2. 山东日照早期的专用煤炭码头。
Coal wharf in Rizhao, Shandong province in the past.

1
—
2

1. 辽宁大连早期的大东港万吨级码头。
10,000-tonne wharf at Dadong port,
Dalian, Liaoning province in the past.

2. 大连港大窑湾集装箱码头。
Dayaowan Container Terminal, Dalian.

成立海南省
Establishment of Hainan Province

1988年4月，七届全国人大一次会议正式批准
设立海南省，划定海南岛为经济特区。
In Apr. 1988, the first session of the 7th National
People's Congress officially approved the
establishment of Hainan province and designated the
Hainan Island as a special economic zone.

1988年4月，海口市数万名群众欢聚在海南省
政府门前，欢庆海南省成立。
In Apr. 1988, tens of thousands of residents
in Haikou gathered in front of the
provincial government of Hainan to celebrate the
establishment.

1

2

1. 1988 年海南省海口市海府路。
Haifu Road, Haikou, Hainan province, 1988.

2. 2018 年海南三亚市。
Sanya, Hainan province, 2018.

以邓小平南方讲话为引领的开放扩大期，促进了面向市场经济体制的一系列根本性改革，打破了姓"资"姓"社"的争论，极大地解放了思想，开启了第二轮改革开放进程。不仅破解了西方的围堵，也让中国经济再上一个新台阶。

Guided by Deng Xiaoping's talks in southern China, the period of expanded opening-up witnessed a series of fundamental reforms oriented towards market economy, settled disputes over capitalism and socialism, greatly liberalized people's mindset and ushered in the second round of reform and opening-up. In this period, China not only broke out of the containment of the West, but also brought its economy onto a higher stage.

第二章　顺势突破（1992—2001）

Chapter 2　The Following Breakthroughs (1992–2001)

邓小平南方视察

Deng Xiaoping's Inspection Tour to Southern China

1992 年初邓小平同志南方讲话，标志着我国进入了扩大开放的新阶段。

At the beginning of 1992, Deng Xiaoping went on an inspection tour to southern China, ushering China into a new stage of expanded opening-up.

不坚持社会主义，不改革开放，不发展经济，不改善人民生活，只能是死路一条。

1. 1992 年作为开放高地的深圳特区。
Shenzhen special zone, China's opening-up highland (1992).

2. 三天一层楼的深圳速度，正是出自于 1985 年建成的深圳国贸大厦。1992 年，邓小平在国贸大厦旋转餐厅发表了著名的南方讲话。
The legend 'Build a floor in three days' （also represented as 'Shenzhen Speed'）is about the Shenzhen International Trade Edifice completed by 1985, where Deng Xiaoping made his famous southern tour speech at the revolving restaurant of building in 1992.

开放 6 个沿江港口城市

Opening up 6 Port Cities by the River

1992 年后，中国相继开放芜湖、九江、黄石、武汉、岳阳、重庆 6 个沿江城市，实行沿海开放城市和地区的经济政策。

Since 1992, China opened up six cities by the Yangtze River one after another, namely, Wuhu, Jiujiang, Huangshi, Wuhan, Yueyang and Chongqing. Economic policies applying to coastal cities and regions opened up earlier were also implemented in these cities.

1
—
2

1. 1992 年正在施工中的重庆朝天门码头。
Chaotianmen wharf under construction, Chongqing, 1992.

2. 1992 年繁忙的武汉港。
The busy port of Wuhan, 1992.

1
2

1. 1993 年已展雄姿的九江长江大桥。
Yangtze River Bridge, Jiujiang,
opened in 1993.

2. 1993 年依江绕湖的芜湖市。
Wuhu, a city surrounded by rivers
and lakes (1993).

开放 14 个沿边城市
Opening up 14 Border Cities

1992 年，中国实施沿边开放战略，陆续批准黑河、绥芬河、珲春、满洲里、二连浩特、伊宁、博乐、塔城、畹町、瑞丽、河口、凭祥、东兴、丹东 14 个城市为沿边开放城市。

In 1992, China began to implement its border opening-up strategy in 14 border cities, namely, Heihe, Suifenhe, Hunchun, Manzhouli, Erenhot, Yining, Bole, Tacheng, Wanding, Ruili, Hekou, Pingxiang, Dongxing and Dandong.

1
2

1. 1992 年俄罗斯卡车司机在满洲里等待验关。
Russian truck drivers waiting for customs inspection in Manzhouli, 1992.

2. 2002 年建成的二连浩特市陆路出入境口岸。
Land port in Erenhot, opened in 2002.

1 |
2

1. 2009 年满载越南产茶叶的货车在东兴边民互市贸易区等待通关。
Lorries laden with Vietnamese tea waiting for customs clearance in the border trade area in Dongxing, 2009.

2. 广西凭祥友谊关，是中国与越南经济、文化交流的一个重要通道。
The Friendship Pass in Pingxiang, Guangxi is a key link for the economic and cultural exchanges between China and Vietnam.

开放 11 个内陆省会城市
Opening up 11 Inland Provincial Capitals

1992 年 6 月，中国决定开放 11 个内陆省会城市。
In Jun. 1992, China decided to open up 11 inland provincial capitals.

1
—
2

1. 2016 年合肥"天鹅湖"。
Swan Lake, Hefei, 2016.

2. 2018 年古城西安。
The ancient city of Xi'an, 2018.

1
2

1. 2017 年，一列动车驶过郑州市区。
A bullet train running through the city of Zhengzhou in 2017.

2. 2018 年长沙梅溪湖城市岛。
Island city, Meixi Lake, Changsha, 2018.

实施西部大开发战略

Implementing the Strategy of Large-scale Development of the Western Region

1999 年 6 月，中国提出要实施西部大开发战略。从此西部地区成为世人关注的开发热土，从经济增速到基础设施，从生态环境到民生改善，享受到西部大开发的丰厚"红利"。

In Jun. 1999, China put forward the strategy of large-scale development of the western region. Since then, the western region has become a development hot land that draws wide attention. It has benefited greatly from the strategy in terms of its economic growth rate, infrastructure construction, ecology and environment as well as improved living standard.

2000 年 8 月，"2000 中国兰州投资贸易洽谈会"在兰州市拉开帷幕。图为外商在会上受到热情接待。

In Aug. 2000, Lanzhou Investment and Trade Fair was held in Lanzhou. Above is a picture of a foreign investor getting warm reception at the fair.

1
2

1. 2000 年 6 月，在"重庆·中国西部开发国际研讨会"上，海内外知名专家学者、国际组织和机构官员、驻华使节等人员研讨西部大开发议题。
In Jun. 2000, guests from home and abroad discussed about China's development of its western region at the Chongqing International Symposium on Development of Western Part of China.

2. 2007 年 1 月，吐峪沟的村民在自己的小院里载歌载舞，欢庆丰收。
In Jan. 2007, villagers in Tuyugou Valley held a party in their yard to celebrate harvests.

以制度性开放为特征的开放深化期，促进了社会主义市场经济体制的巩固和完善。2001 年中国加入世贸组织后，国有企业改革加快，民营经济迅速发展，金融体制、投资体制等改革全面推开，中国经济增长开启了新的周期。

Deepening the institutionalized opening-up policy further consolidates and improves the socialist market economy. Since China's WTO accession in 2001, reform of state-owned enterprises (SOE) has accelerated. The private sector has been growing rapidly. Reform of the financial and investment systems has been carried out extensively. China has entered a new economic growth cycle.

第三章 融入世界（2001—2012）
Chapter 3   Integration into the World (2001–2012)

加入世贸组织
WTO Accession

2001 年 12 月，我国正式成为世贸组织 (WTO) 第 143 个成员。
In Dec. 2001, China officially became the 143rd member of the WTO.

2001 年 11 月 11 日，时任中国外经贸部部长石广生代表中国政府在《中国加入世贸组织议定书》上签字。12 月 11 日，中国成为世贸组织成员。
On Nov.11 2001, then Minister of Foreign Trade and Economic Cooperation, Shi Guangsheng, signed the *Protocol on China's Accession to the World Trade Organization (WTO)* on behalf of the Chinese government. China officially became a member of the WTO on Dec.11, 2001.

中国切实履行加入世贸组织承诺

货物贸易

● **全面降低关税**
关税总水平由2001年的15.3%降至9.8%
工业品平均税率由14.8%降至8.9%，其中汽车关税2006年7月1日降至25%
农业品平均税率由23.2%降至15.2%

● **取消非关税措施**
取消进口配额、进口许可证和特定招标等非关税措施，涉及汽车、机电

产品、天然橡胶等424个税号产品
对小麦、玉米、大米、食糖、棉花、羊毛、毛条和化肥等大宗商品实行关税配额管理

● **全面放开对外贸易经营权**

服务贸易

● **电信服务**
2001年，基础电信、增值电信允许外资进入
2003年，增值电信取消地域限制
2006年，移动话音和数据服务取消地域限制
2007年，基础电信其他业务取消地域限制

● **银行服务**
2001年，允许外国金融机构在中国提供外汇服务
2003年，允许外国金融机构向中国企业提供人民币本币业务
2006年，允许外国金融机构向所有中国客户提供服务
2006年，取消外资股比、设立形式和地域限制

● **保险服务**
2001年，允许设立非寿验分公司和合资寿险、非寿险公司
2003年，允许设立独资非寿险子公司
2004年，取消地域限制
2005年，取消强制分保要求
2006年，允许设立独资保险经纪子公司

● **证券服务**
2001年，允许设立合资证券投资基金管理公司
2004年，允许设立合资证券公司

● **视听服务**
2001年，允许设立中外合作音像制品分销企业

2001年，允许每年以分账形式进口20部外国电影
2001年，允许外商建设和/或改造电影院

● **分销服务**
2001年，允许外资从事零售业务
2002年，允许外资从事佣金代理和批发业务
2004年，取消外资参与特许经营的限制
2006年，取消外资从事一般分销业务的股比限制

● **教育服务（不包括义务及特殊教育）**
2001年，允许中外合作办学，外方可获多数拥有权

● **速递服务（不包括邮政专营服务）**
2001年，允许外资从事速递服务
2002年，允许外资控股
2005年，允许设立独资子公司

● **建筑及相关工程服务**
2001年，允许设立合资企业，外资可控股
2004年，允许设立独资企业

● **环境服务**
2001年，允许设立合资企业，外资可控股

知识产权

2014年，在北京、上海、广州成立3家知识产权法院
2018年，在南京、苏州、武汉、西安等15个中级法院中设立知识产权专门审判机构
2017年，对外支付知识产权费达到286亿美元，加入之后年均增长17%
2017年，积极推动《修改<与贸易有关的知识产权协定>议定书》正式生效，该议定书是世贸组织成立以来首次成功修改的现有协定

● **专利**
2000年，第二次修正《专利法》，全面遵守《TRIPS协定》相关规定
2008年，第三次修正《专利法》，进一步提升保护水平
2001年至2017年，中国专利的申请量由20万件增长到138万件，位居全球第一位；国外来华专利申请量由3.3万件增长到13.6万件，增长了3.3倍

● **商标**
2001年，第二次修正《商标法》，全面遵守《TRIPS协定》相关规定
2013年，第三次修正《商标法》，增加了惩罚性赔偿制度
2001年至2017年，中国商标的申请量由27万件增长到574万件，位居全球第一位

● **版权**
2001年，第一次修正《著作权法》，全面遵守《TRIPS协定》相关规定
2010年，第二次修正《著作权法》，进一步提升保护水平

● **地理标识（包括原产地名称）**
2001年，加入时已遵守《TRIPS协定》有关规定

● **工业设计**
2001年，加入时已遵守《TRIPS协定》有关规定

● **植物新品种保护**
2013年，第一次修订《植物新品种保护条例》
2014年，第二次修订《植物新品种保护条例》

● **集成电路布图设计**
2001年，《集成电路布图设计保护条例》施行

● **未披露信息**
2017年，第一次修订《反不正当竞争法》，进一步完善商业秘密的保护
我国也将商业秘密纳入《刑法》保护范围

中国主动降低汽车进口关税并取消进口配额管理，整车进口数量由 1980 年 5.11 万辆增加到 2017 年 124.65 万辆。图为天津港进口汽车滚装码头。
China voluntarily reduced auto import duties and removed import quotas, which drove up whole car imports from 51,100 units of 1980 to 1.2465 million units of 2017. The picture shows the automobile Ro–Ro terminal at the Port of Tianjin.

离境退税

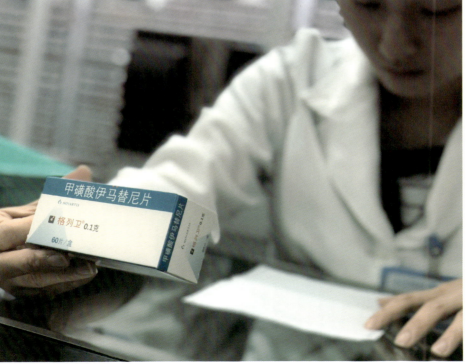

甲磺酸伊马替尼片

格列卫 0.1克

60片/盒

1
2

1. 2015 年 7 月，北京市率先在全国实施境外旅客购物离境退税。
In Jul. 2015, Beijing became China's first city to process tax refunds for overseas visitors.

2. 2018 年 5 月起，包括抗癌药在内的 28 项药品的进口关税降为零，已有多种抗癌药进入医保目录。图为广东省人民医院药师遵照医嘱核对抗癌药物。
Starting from May 2018, 28 imported drugs are duty-free when imported into China, including anti-cancer drugs, several of which are included in the reimbursement drug lists. The picture shows a pharmacist of Guangdong Provincial People's Hospital checking anti-cancer drugs against the prescription.

改革管理体制
Foreign Trade Regime Reform

2004年4月，十届全国人大常务委员会八次会议修订通过新的《对外贸易法》。外贸经营权放开，由审批改为备案登记制。

The Eighth Meeting of the 10th NPC Standing Committee revised and ratified the new *Foreign Trade Law* in Apr. 2004. Foreign trade dealers only need to register with the authority responsible, and no longer have to ask for approval from the Chinese government.

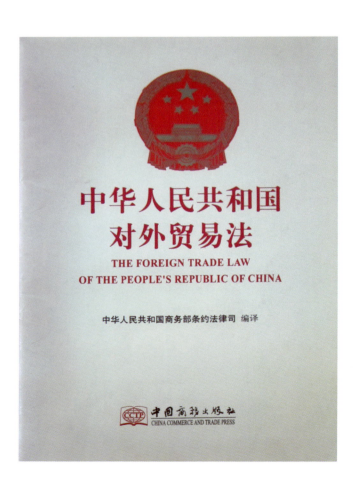

1. 2004年7月，马先生第一个领取北京对外贸易经营者企业登记表。
Mr. Ma was the first dealer in Beijing to receive the foreign trade registration form in Jul. 2004.

2.《对外贸易法》文本封面。
Front cover of the *Foreign Trade Law*.

1
2

2003 年 3 月，十届全国人大一次会议批准国务院将原对外贸易经济合作部组建为商务部，主管国内外贸易和国际经济合作。

In Mar. 2003, the First Session of the 10th NPC approved of reorganizing the Ministry of Foreign Trade and Economic Cooperation as the Ministry of Commerce (MOFCOM) under the State Council of China. MOFCOM is responsible for domestic and foreign trade, and international economic cooperation.

1. 原对外贸易经济合作部门牌。
The building sign of the Ministry of Foreign Trade and Economic Cooperation in the picture above.

2. 商务部门牌。
The building sign of the Ministry of Commerce in the picture below.

清理法律法规
Sorting out Laws and Regulations

加入世贸组织前后，中央政府部门和地方政府多次清理地方性法规、政府规章和其他政策措施。这是中国有史以来最大规模的法律文件清理活动。

Before and after joining the World Trade Organization, the central government and local governments have straightened out local regulations, departmental rules and other policy measures many a time. The scale of legal documents sorted out is the largest one China has ever seen.

```
  |   1
--+------
2 |   3
```

1. 商务部历年法律法规清理活动内容。
Laws and regulations MOFCOM has sorted out in the previous years.

2. 2000—2016 年，多次修订《中华人民共和国外资企业法》《中华人民共和国中外合作经营企业法》《中华人民共和国中外合资经营企业法》。
From 2000 to 2016, multiple revisions were made to the *Law on Foreign Capital Enterprises,* the *Law on Chinese-Foreign Contractual Joint Ventures,* and the *Law on Chinese-Foreign Equity Joint Ventures.*

3. 2004—2018 年，多次修订《外商投资产业指导目录》。
From 2004 to 2018, multiple revisions were made to the *Catalogue for the Guidance of Foreign Investment Industries.*

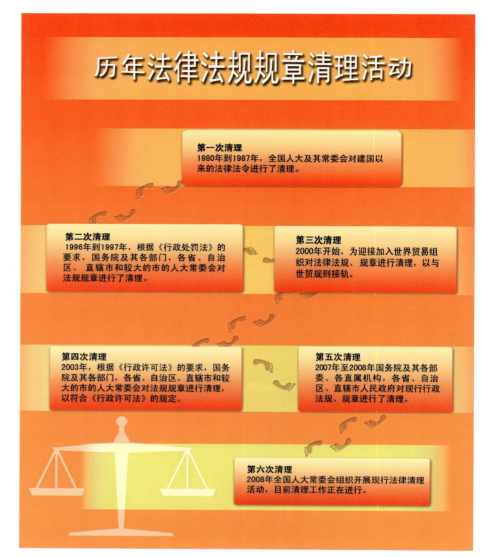

历年法律法规规章清理活动

第一次清理
1980年到1987年，全国人大及其常委会对建国以来的法律法令进行了清理。

第二次清理
1996年到1997年，根据《行政处罚法》的要求，国务院及其各部门，各省、自治区、直辖市和较大的市的人大常委会对法规规章进行了清理。

第三次清理
2000年开始，为迎接加入世界贸易组织对法律法规、规章进行清理，以与世贸规则接轨。

第四次清理
2003年，根据《行政许可法》的要求，国务院及其各部门，各省、自治区、直辖市和较大的市的人大常委会对法规规章进行清理，以符合《行政许可法》的规定。

第五次清理
2007年至2008年国务院及其各部委、各直属机构，各省、自治区、直辖市人民政府对现行行政法规、规章进行了清理。

第六次清理
2008年全国人大常委会组织开展现行法律清理活动，目前清理工作正在进行。

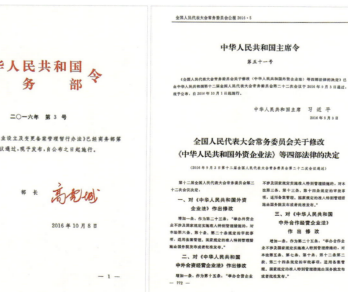

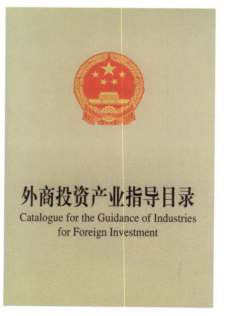

外商投资产业指导目录
Catalogue for the Guidance of Industries for Foreign Investment

接受贸易政策审议
Trade Policy Reviews

2006—2018 年，中国全面、深入、高效地接受了世贸组织七次贸易政策审议。

From 2006 to 2018, China has fully undergone seven WTO trade policy reviews which were extensive and highly efficient.

1
2

1. 2006 年 4 月　首次世贸组织中国贸易政策审议现场。
The 1st Trade Folicy Review of China in Apr. 2006.

2. 2018 年 7 月，第七次世贸组织中国贸易政策审议现场。
The 7th Trade Policy Review of China in Jul. 2018.

扩大服务业开放
Further Liberalizing Service Sector

中国服务领域开放承诺全部履行完毕。中国承诺开放9大类100个分部门，接近发达成员平均承诺开放108个分部门的水平，远高于发展中成员平均承诺开放26个分部门的水平。
China's commitments to opening up services sector have all been fulfilled. China has committed to open 100 subsectors in nine categories, while developed members committed to open 108 subsectors on average. China has far exceeded the average level of commitment of developing members which are 26 subsectors.

1	3
2	

1. 2003年5月，中国允许外商在中国投资出版物分销企业。图为外国记者在北京书报亭浏览境外报刊。
Foreign investors are allowed to invest in sub-distribution of publications in China since May. 2003. In the picture, a foreign journalist is reading foreign newspaper at a newsstand in Beijing.

2. 2004年成立的宁波诺丁汉大学是中国第一所中外合作创办的高等院校。图为宁波诺丁汉大学首届毕业典礼。
University of Nottingham Ningbo China (UNNC), established in 2004, was the first Sino-foreign University to open its doors in China. The picture shows the first graduation ceremony in the University of Nottingham Ningbo.

3. 扩大服务贸易开放领域。2006年12月，中国取消对外资银行的一切非审慎性市场准入限制。图为上海陆家嘴金融区一角。
The Regulation on Administration of Foreign-funded Banks entered into force in Dec. 2006. China removed non-prudent market access restrictions on foreign-invested banks. The picture shows Lujiazui financial district.

进入世贸组织核心层
Becoming Core Member of the WTO

经过多年的努力，中国已成为世贸组织决策圈的核心成员，从国际贸易规则的跟随者逐步成为参与者、建设者、贡献者。

China has become one of the core WTO members in decision-making after years of hard work. Instead of being a mere follower of international trading rules, we are now involved in the rule-making in a constructive way.

2008 年 7 月，中国首次进入世贸组织规则制定的核心层，中国代表在日内瓦世贸组织总部出席小型部长会议。

China attended the Mini-ministerial Conference in WTO headquarters in Geneva in Jul. 2008, marking its first involvement in rule-making as a core member.

推进新区开放

Promoting Opening Up in New Areas

自上海浦东新区之后，中国相继设立天津滨海新区和重庆两江新区，形成东中西部协调发展的新格局。

China has set up Tianjin Binhai New Area and Chongqing Liangjiang New Area since the establishment of Pudong New Area in Shanghai, forming a new landscape of coordinated development in east, middle and west China.

2005 年 10 月，中共十六届五中全会作出将天津滨海新区开发开放纳入国家发展战略布局的重大决策。

In Oct. 2005, the Fifth Plenary Session of the 16th CPC Central Committee decided to include development and opening up of Tianjin Binhai New Area in national development strategy plans.

2010 年 5 月，国务院正式批准设立重庆两江新区并赋予其五大功能定位。
In May. 2010, the State Council approved the proposal for Chongqing Liangjiang New Area and identified its five functions.

以"一带一路"及高水平开放为特征的开放引领期，增添了新时代全面深化改革的新动力。2012年十八大召开后，我国以"一带一路"为顶层设计，以新一轮高水平开放为战略举措，以开放型世界经济为合作愿景，推动我国对外开放再上一个新台阶。

The Belt and Road Initiative and other high-level opening up measures create new driving force for comprehensively deepening reform in the new era. Since the 18th CPC National Congress in 2012, China has followed the Belt and Road Initiative, taken strategic measures of high-level opening up, and pushed for building an open world economy, thus scaling new heights in the opening up agenda.

第四章 鼎新图强（2012年至今）
Chapter 4 Reform to Be Strong (2012-now)

十八大胜利召开
The 18th National Congress of the CPC

2012年11月，中国共产党第十八次全国代表大会在人民大会堂召开，确定全面建成小康社会和全面深化改革开放的目标，作出了系列改革开放的重大举措。

The 18th National Congress of the CPC convened in the Grand Hall of the People in Nov. 2012, setting the goal of completing the building of a moderately prosperous society in all respects and comprehensively deepening reform and opening up. A host of major measures were announced to achieve the goal.

中共十八大会议现场。
The venue of the 18th CPC National Congress.

1
2

1. 2017 年 10 月，商务部等 13 部门颁布《关于复制推广构建开放型经济新体制综合试点经验的通知》。图为试点城市济南市的齐鲁软件园。
MOFCOM and other 12 ministries and departments issued the *Notice on Replicating and Applying Experience of Pilot Free Trade Zones in Building the New System of Open Economy* in Oct. 2017. The picture shows the Qilu Software Park in the pilot city of Jinan.

2. 东莞松山湖科技产业园区。
Dongguan Songshan Lake Science and Technology Industrial Park.

武汉城市圈依托铁路通道，加快建设全国高铁快递转运分拨中心。
Based on rail links, Wuhan Metropolitan Area steps up efforts to build the transfer and sorting center for national high-speed train delivery.

设立首个中国自由贸易试验区
Setting up the First Pilot Free Trade Zone in China

2013 年 8 月，党中央、国务院批准设立中国（上海）自由贸易试验区。

In Aug. 2013, the State Council approved the plan to establish China (Shanghai) Pilot Free Trade Zone.

中国（上海）自由贸易试验区标识。

The sign of Shanghai Pilot Free Trade Zone in Shanghai Waigaoqiao Bonded Zone.

设立第二批中国自由贸易试验区

The Second Batch of Pilot Free Trade Zones in China

2015 年 4 月，广东、天津、福建 3 个自由贸易试验区挂牌成立。
In Apr. 2015, the State Council approved launching three pilot free trade zones in Tianjin, Fujian and Guangdong respectively.

1
2
3

1. 位于天津空港经济区中心大道的中国（天津）自由贸易试验区标识。
The sign of Tianjin Pilot Free Trade Zone in Konggang Economic Development Zone.

2. 中国（福建）自由贸易试验区福州出口加工区的进口商品展示直销中心关口。
The demonstration and direct sale center for imported goods in the export processing zone of China (Fujian) Pilot Free Trade Zone.

3. 中国（广东）自由贸易试验区深圳前海蛇口片区。
Shekou area in Qianhai of Shenzhen in China (Guangdong) Pilot Free Trade Zone.

设立第三批自由贸易试验区

The Third Batch of Pilot Free Trade Zones in China

2017 年 4 月，中国第三批 7 个自由贸易试验区正式挂牌，它们分别是辽宁、浙江、河南、湖北、重庆、四川、陕西自由贸易试验区。

In Apr. 2017, China launched the third batch of seven pilot free trade zones in Liaoning, Zhejiang, Henan, Hubei, Chongqing, Sichuan, and Shaanxi respectively.

1

2

1. 中国（辽宁）自由贸易试验区大连片区。
Dalian area in China (Liaoning) Pilot Free Trade Zone.

2. 中国（浙江）自由贸易试验区位于舟山的试验区标识。
The sign of China (Zhejiang) Pilot Free Trade Zone in Zhoushan.

1
2

1. 2017 年 4 月，中国（河南）自由贸易试验区挂牌成立。
In Apr. 2017, China (Henan) Pilot Free Trade Zone was established.

2. 2017 年 4 月，中国（湖北）自由贸易试验区在武汉挂牌成立。
In Apr. 2017, China (Hubei) Pilot Free Trade Zone was launched in Wuhan.

1. 2017 年 4 月，中国（重庆）自由贸
易试验区挂牌成立。
In Apr. 2017, China (Chongqing) Pilot
Free Trade Zone was established.

2. 2017 年 4 月，中国（四川）自由贸
易试验区挂牌成立。
In Apr. 2017, China (Sichuan) Pilot
Free Trade Zone was established.

2017 年 4 月，中国（陕西）自由贸易试
验区挂牌成立。
In Apr. 2017, China (Shaanxi) Pilot Free
Trade Zone was established.

十九大胜利召开
The 19th National Congress of the CPC

2017 年 10 月，中国共产党第十九次全国代表大会在人民大会堂召开，提出要推动形成全面开放新格局，发展更高层次的开放型经济，推动建设开放型世界经济。

The 19th CPC National Congress held in the Great Hall of the People in Oct. 2017 proposed to create a new landscape of comprehensive opening up, cultivate an open economy at a higher level, and build an open world economy.

商务部党组认真传达学习贯彻党的十九大精神。
The Party Leadership Group of MOFCOM urges officials to study and implement the spirit of the 19th National Congress of the CPC.

1

2

1. 2018年9月，国务院批复同意设立中国（海南）自由贸易试验区，支持海南逐步探索、稳步推进中国特色自由贸易港建设。图为海南洋浦保税港区。

In Sep. 2018, the State Council approved the establishment of China (Hainan) Pilot Free Trade Zone and to progressively explore and build a free trade port with Chinese characteristics. Above is the picture of Yangpu bonded port zone in Hainan.

2. 2018年9月，钟山部长与海南省委副书记、省长沈晓明签署部省合作协议。

In Sep. 2018, Zhong Shan, Minister of Commerce, and Shen Xiaoming, Deputy Secretary of CPC Hainan Provincial Committee and Governor of Hainan, signed the cooperation agreement between MOFCOM and Hainan Province.

展望未来，中国商务人将继续肩扛使命，在改革开放的路上不懈前行。"莫听穿林打叶声，何妨吟啸且徐行。"无论什么样的风雨，都无法阻挡中国人民奔向美好生活的脚步。改革开放只有进行时。

Part IV   An Economic and Trading Powerhouse

Looking into the future, Chinese commerce workers will remain committed to the mission and keep Marching down the path of reform and opening up. 'Pay no attention to the rain falling in the woods patting leaves and why not chant while going slowly?' As the line from an ancient Chinese poem suggests, no wind and rain could stop the Chinese people from pursuing a good life. Reform and opening up is an ongoing process.

第一章　奋斗目标
Chapter 1　Goal of Struggle

分三阶段，努力提前建成经贸强国。
Efforts are made by three stages to build a trade and economic powerhouse ahead of time.

2018 年 3 月，在十三届全国人大一次会议上，商务部部长钟山、副部长兼国际贸易谈判副代表王受文、副部长钱克明就"推动形成全面开放新格局 推动商务事业高质量发展"相关问题回答中外记者提问。商务部提出了建设经贸强国、推动商务高质量发展的总体思路和具体措施，概括起来是"一个奋斗目标、六项主要任务和八大行动计划"总体构想。

In Mar. 2018, at the 1st Session of the 13th National People's Congress, Minister Zhong Shan, Vice Minister and Deputy CITR Wang Shouwen and Vice Minister Qian Keming of Commerce took questions from the press at home and abroad on "Pushing for a New Landscape of Comprehensive Opening up and Promoting the Quality Development of the Commerce Cause". MOFCOM sets out general guidelines and specific measures for building an economic and trading powerhouse and promoting quality commerce development, in short, the master program of "one goal, six tasks and eight action plans".

奋斗目标
努力提前建成经贸强国

2050年前
全面建成经贸强国

2035年前
基本建成经贸强国

2020年前
进一步巩固经贸大国地位

第二章　主要任务

Chapter 2　Main Tasks

从六个方面，努力完成既定任务。
Set tasks will be met in six aspects.

第三章 行动计划
Chapter 3 Action Plans

从八个领域，制订 150 条措施，推动商务高质量发展。
Action plans with 150 points have been drawn up in eight areas to promote quality commerce development.

消费升级行动计划
Plans for Consumption Upgrade

实施商圈消费引领工程。图为被誉为"中国电子第一街"的深圳华强北商圈。
Implementing the Business Circle Consumption Guidance Program: The picture above shows Shenzhen Huaqiangbei Business Circle, which is known as China's No.1 electronics street.

1. 推动绿色消费。图为 2018 年 6 月，西安比亚迪纯电动客车基地工人在测量客车轮眉高度。
Promoting green consumption: In Jun. 2018, workers measuring the height of wheel brow at the BYD electric vehicle base in Xi'an.

2. 打造城乡便民消费服务中心。图为 2018 年 8 月，一家三口在智慧小镇的"智慧零售体验馆"里选购商品。
Setting up urban and rural consumer service centers: In Aug. 2018, a family of three shopping in the Smart Retail Experience Booth in a smart town.

构建现代供应链。盒马鲜生作为新零售类型的领头羊体验店，将线上和线下打通，实现全渠道营销和交易模式。图为盒马鲜生餐厨操作间。
Creating modern supply chains: As a pioneer of new retail, Hema store links on-line and off-line experience for all-channel marketing and trading. The picture shows a kitchen operating room of a Hema store.

贸易强国行动计划
Plans for a Trading Powerhouse

1. 任鸿斌部长助理巡视第 124 届广交会展馆并调研参展企业。
Assistant Minister Ren Hongbin inspected the 124th Canton Fair and held discussions with companies represented.

2. 推进贸易便利化。图为 2018 年 10 月，工作人员介绍中国（上海）国际贸易"单一窗口"的相关情况。
Advancing trade facilitation: In Oct. 2018, staff introducing the China (Shanghai) Single Window for International Trade.

2015 年以来，国务院设立了 35 个跨境电子商务综合试验区。图片为杭州综试区跨贸小镇和深圳综试区蛇口网谷。

Since 2015, the State Council has set up 35 Cross-Border E-commerce Comprehensive Pilot Areas (hereinafter referred to as Comprehensive Pilot Area). The pictures show the Cross-border Trading Town of Hangzhou Comprehensive Pilot Area and the Shekou Net Valley of Shenzhen Comprehensive Pilot Area.

观众通过天桥进入进博会场馆。
Visitors accessing the CIIE venue through the overpass.

首届中国国际进口博览会暨虹桥国际经贸论坛

THE FIRST CHINA INTERNATIONAL IMPORT EXPO AND THE HONGQIAO INTERNATIONAL ECONOMIC AND TRADE FORUM

开幕式
OPENING CEREMONY

2018年11月5日
November 5th, 2018

中国·上海
Shanghai, China

2018年11月，首届中国国际进口博览会暨虹桥国际经贸论坛在上海举行。图为国际货币基金组织总裁拉加德演讲。
In Nov. 2018, the 1st China International Import Expo and the Hongqiao International Economic and Trade Forum was held in Shanghai. The picture above shows IMF Managing Director Lagarde delivering a speech.

外资促进行动计划
Plans for Promoting FDI

1
2

1. 推进金融业开放。图为第十一届中国企业国际融资洽谈会——科技国际融资洽谈会（融洽会）在天津开幕。
Promoting financial liberalization: The 11th China International Private Equity Forum—the Scientific and Technological Private Equity Forum (CIPEF) opened in Tianjin.

2. 提高西部地区吸收外资规模和质量。图为2018成都国际投资峰会在世纪城新国际会展中心举行。
Enhancing the scale and quality of FDI in the western region: 2018 Chengdu International Investment Summit was held at the Chengdu Century City New International Convention and Exhibition Center.

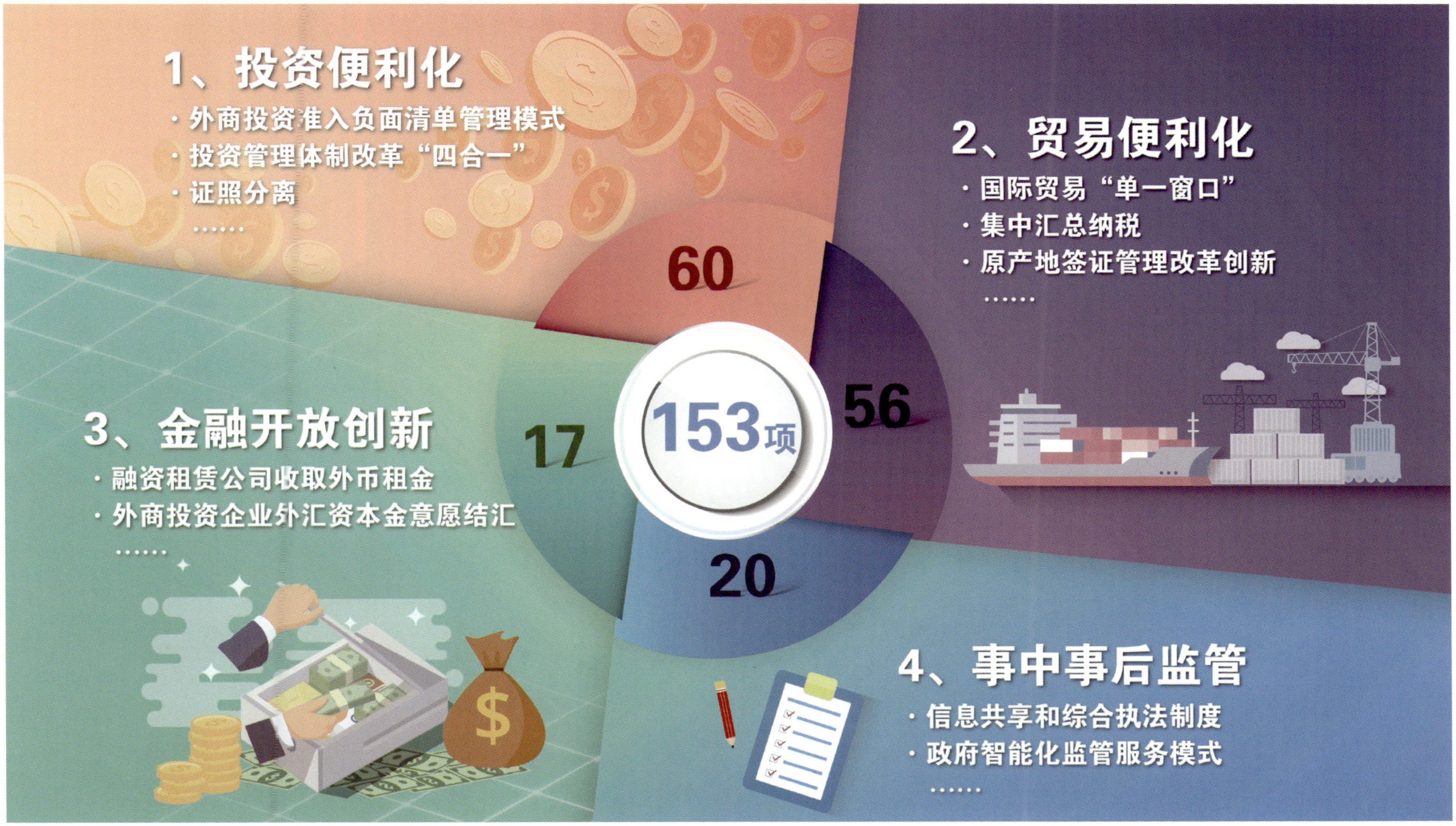

1、投资便利化
· 外商投资准入负面清单管理模式
· 投资管理体制改革"四合一"
· 证照分离
· ……

2、贸易便利化
· 国际贸易"单一窗口"
· 集中汇总纳税
· 原产地签证管理改革创新
· ……

3、金融开放创新
· 融资租赁公司收取外币租金
· 外商投资企业外汇资本金意愿结汇
· ……

4、事中事后监管
· 信息共享和综合执法制度
· 政府智能化监管服务模式
· ……

60
56
153项
17
20

截至 2018 年底，自由贸易试验区总结形成了 153 项改革试点经验在全国推广，带动了全国范围内营商环境不断优化，充分发挥了"试验田"作用。
By the end of 2018, the FTZs had summarized reform pilots into 153 pieces of experience for national rollout, driving the continuous optimization of national business environment and giving full play to the role of "testing ground".

对外投资创新行动计划
Plans for ODI Innovation

支持自主品牌企业对外投资。图为 2018 年 5 月，首辆中国自主品牌汽车在阿尔及利亚塞提夫省工业园下线。
Supporting the outbound investment of domestic brands: In May. 2018, the first Chinese-branded vehicles were launched in an industrial park in Setif, Algeria.

推动企业联合走出去。2018 年 4 月，中国华为公司设在巴黎的开放实验室正式启用。
Pushing for coordinated going global: In Apr. 2018, Huawei's open lab in Paris was officialy launched.

援外综合效益提升行动计划
Plans for Improving the Synergetic Benefits of Foreign Assistance

1. 2018 年 8 月，在位于利比里亚首都蒙罗维亚市郊的中国援利竹藤编培训中心，中国师傅教授当地学员制作家具。
In Aug. 2018, at the China–Aided Bamboo and Rattan Weaving Training Center in the suburbs of Monrovia, capital of Liberia, a Chinese master is teaching a local student to make furniture.

2. 中国助力卢旺达技术人才培养。图为 2018 年 8 月，中国政府援建的卢旺达穆桑泽职业技术学校的学生正在做毕业设计。
China lends help to Rwanda's talent training program: In Aug. 2018, students of the China–aided Musanze Polytechnic in Rwanda are working on their graduation design.

1
2

2018 年 10 月，中国援莫赛赛机场项目奠基仪式在莫桑比克加扎省赛赛市隆重举行。
In Oct. 2018, the grand foundation stone laying ceremony for the China-aided Xai-Xai airport was held in Xai-Xai, Gaza of Mozambique.

"一带一路"合作行动计划
Plans for Belt and Road Cooperation

2018 年 11 月，在首届中国国际进口博览会期间，商务部和湖北省人民政府在上海共同举办中国—北欧经贸合作论坛。
In Nov. 2018, during the 1st CIIE, MOFCOM and the Hubei Provincial People's Government co-organized the China-Nordic Trade and Economic Cooperation Forum in Shanghai.

1. 2018年6月，香港举办第三届"一带一路"高峰论坛。图为参会嘉宾在进行洽谈交流。
In Jun. 2018, Hong Kong hosted the 3rd Belt and Road Summit Forum. The picture shows participants in one–on–one meetings.

2. 2018年10月，首届"一带一路"非中艺术交流展暨非中文化论坛在中国国家图书馆举行。
In Oct. 2018, the 1st Belt and Road China–Africa Art Exchange Exhibition and China–Africa Culture Forum were held in the National Library of China.

多边区域经贸合作行动计划
Plans for Multilateral and Regional Trade and Economic Cooperation

1. 2018 年 9 月，中国政府发布《关于中美经贸摩擦的事实与中方立场》白皮书。
In Sept. 2018, the Chinese government published a white paper of *The Facts and China's Position on China–US Trade Friction*.

2. 中国积极推进《区域全面经济伙伴关系协定》（RCEP）谈判。图为 2016 年 10 月，RCEP 第 15 轮谈判在天津举行。
China actively pushes forward the negotiations of *Regional Comprehensive Economic Partnership*: in Oct. 2016, the 15th round of RCEP negotiations was held in Tianjin.

1

2

经贸强国
An Economic and Trading Powerhouse
40周年

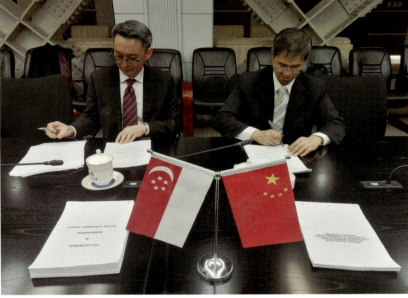

1 | 2
—————
3 |

1. 中国—以色列自贸区第四轮谈判情景。
The picture was taken during the 4th round of China–Israel FTA talks.

2. 中新双方进行中国—新加坡自贸协定升级议定书文本的最后审核。
Both sides were carrying out the final check on China–Singapore Free Trade Agreement Upgrade Protocol.

3. 推动与巴基斯坦自贸协定第二阶段谈判，图为双方代表正在进行磋商。
Second phase of FTA negotiations with Pakistan: teams from the two sides in talks.

商务扶贫行动计划
Plans for Poverty Alleviation through Commerce

2018 年 10 月，钟山部长率队赴商务部定点扶贫县湖南省城步苗族自治县开展扶贫调研，深入 4 个贫困村实地考察了商务扶贫项目，看望慰问了建档立卡贫困户，走访了致富带头人，并召开定点扶贫工作座谈会。

In Oct. 2018, Minister Zhong Shan headed a team to MOFCOM's pair-up recipient Chengbu Miao-Ethnic Autonomous County, Hunan Province for poverty alleviation research, visiting commerce-driven poverty alleviation projects in four poor villages, comforted registered poor households, called at getting-rich leaders and held a poverty alleviation meeting.

```
1 | 2
-----
  3
```

1. 广安群策村柚农分红大会现场。
Dividends sharing for grapefruit growers in Qunce Village, Guang'an.

2. 贫困户家门前的一户一码，实现扶贫"精准化"管理。
QR codes on the doors of poor households enable precision management for poverty alleviation.

3. 李成钢部长助理在湖南省城步县调研扶贫产业食用菌种植。
Assistant Minister Li Chenggang investigated the poverty alleviation industry of edible fungi cultivation in Chengbu County, Hunan Province.

后　记

　　四十年改革开放带来的沧桑巨变是每一个中国人都能真切感受到的。这场伟大变革不仅改变着中国，也影响着世界。

　　改革开放的成果令人瞩目，在庆祝的同时，我们也要清醒地认识到，前方仍存在着困难与挑战。习近平总书记在中国国际进口博览会开幕式的主旨演讲中指出："只要我们保持战略定力，全面深化改革开放，深化供给侧结构性改革，下大气力解决存在的突出矛盾和问题，中国经济就一定能加快转入高质量发展轨道，中国人民就一定能战胜前进道路上的一切困难挑战，中国就一定能迎来更加光明的发展前景。"

　　"艰难困苦，玉汝于成"。经历了五千年的绵延不绝，百余年的救亡图存，近七十年的不懈奋斗，四十年的开放发展，中国推动更高水平开放的脚步不会停滞！中国推动建设开放型世界经济的脚步不会停滞！中国推动构建人类命运共同体的脚步不会停滞！

Epilogue

The transformation brought by reform and opening up over the past forty years is palpable to everyone in China, which has not only changed China, but also sent reverberations across the world.

While celebrating the phenomenal success of reform and opening up, we must be well aware of the difficulties and challenges lying ahead. President Xi Jinping pointed out at the China International Import Expo, "As long as we have strategic confidence, deepen reform and opening-up across the board, intensify supply-side structural reforms and make greater efforts to solve outstanding problems, then the Chinese economy will surely make a quicker transition to high-quality development, the Chinese people will surely overcome all challenges coming our way, and China will surely embrace a brighter future of development."

As the saying goes, difficulty is the nurse of greatness. Following an uninterrupted history of more than five thousand years, over a century's struggle for national survival, nearly seventy years' relentless efforts and four decades of open development, China's pursuit for higher-level opening up will not stop, its push for an open world economy will not stop, and its quest for a community of shared future for mankind will not stop.